TAPESTRY

PATTERNS OF CULTURAL IDENTITY

TAPESTRY

The **Tapestry** program of language materials is based on the concepts presented in ***The Tapestry of Language Learning:*** *The Individual in the Communicative Classroom* by Robin C. Scarcella & Rebecca L. Oxford.

❖

Each title in this program focuses on:

❖

Individual learner strategies and instruction

❖

The relatedness of skills

❖

Ongoing self-assessment

❖

Authentic material as input

❖

Theme-based learning linked to task-based instruction

❖

Attention to all aspects of communicative competence

TAPESTRY

PATTERNS OF CULTURAL IDENTITY

Rebecca L. Oxford

I(T)P

Heinle & Heinle Publishers
An International Thomson Publishing Company
Boston, Massachusetts, 02116, USA

The publication of *Patterns of Cultural Identity* was directed by the members of the Heinle & Heinle Global Innovations Publishing Team:

Elizabeth Holthaus, Global Innovations Team Leader
David C. Lee, Editorial Director
John F. McHugh, Market Development Director
Lisa McLaughlin, Production Services Coordinator

Also participating in the publication of this program were:

Publisher: Stanley J. Galek
Director of Production: Elizabeth Holthaus
Assistant Editor: Kenneth Mattsson
Manufacturing Coordinator: Mary Beth Hennebury
Full Service Project Manager/Compositor: PC&F, Inc.
Interior Design: Maureen Lauran
Cover Design: Maureen Lauran

Manufactured in the United States of America

ISBN 0-8384-4123-8

Heinle & Heinle Publishers is an International Thomson Publishing Company.

10 9 8 7 6 5 4 3 2 1

To Linda Ward Burgess
for her deep cultural insights
and generosity,

and to my husband,
Maury Breecher
for his love and support

PHOTO CREDITS

1, Tony Stone Images; 2, left, Anna Zuckerman/PhotoEdit; 2, center, SuperStock; 2, right, SuperStock; 4, left, Robert Brenner/PhotoEdit; 4, right, Murray & Associates/Tony Stone; 10, courtesy of Ashraf el Sayed and Amany Saleh; 13, courtesy of Elizabeth Atcheson; 16, courtesy of JoAn D. Criddle; 27, courtesy of Rebecca L. Oxford and Young Ye Park-Oh; 33, Telegraph Colour Library/FPG International; 35, Dennis O'Clair/Tony Stone Images; 50, Robert Brenner/PhotoEdit; 55, left, M. Fritz/SuperStock; 55, right, © Blaine Harrington III/The Stock Market; 59, courtesy of Maury M. Breecher; 67, Michael Newman/PhotoEdit; 68, left, © Allen Lee Page/The Stock Market; 68, right, SuperStock; 76, Marc Pokempner/Tony Stone Images; 77, Chip Henderson/Tony Stone Images; 94, Reuters/Bettmann; 101, Myrleen Ferguson Cate/PhotoEdit; 111, Lionel Delevingne/Stock, Boston; 116, Bill Bachmann/PhotoEdit; 120, courtesy of Rebecca Oxford; 128, courtesy of U.S. Rep. Dan Burton and *People Weekly*.

ART CREDITS

19, Cartoon from *Pasajes: Actividades.* Copyright © 1987 by McGraw-Hill, Inc. Reprinted by permission of McGraw-Hill, Inc.
46, Doonesbury cartoon. Used with permission of Universal Press Syndicate.
47, Rose Is Rose cartoon. Reprinted by permission of UFS, Inc.
53, Minimal acceptable distance between parent and teenager in public. From *Dave Barry's Only Travel Guide You'll Ever Need* by Dave Barry. Copyright © 1989 by Dave Barry. Reprinted by permission of Ballantine Books, a division of Random House, Inc.
105, Tiny's Diner cartoon on family values. *News for You,* 1992. Copyright © New Reader's Press. Used by permission.

TEXT CREDITS

7, Task 1.7 contains some concepts adapted from Robert Moran. In William H. Weeks, Paul B. Pedersen, and Richard W. Brislin, eds., *A Manual of Structured Experiences for Cross-Cultural Learning.* Yarmouth, ME: Intercultural Press, 1990.
8–9, Iceberg concept is adapted from Edward T. Hall, "The Cultural Iceberg" in *The Hidden Dimension.* Garden City, New York: Anchor Books, 1969.
11 (also tape and tapescript), "Ashraf and Sayed Deal with U.S. Culture," by Ashraf el Sayed. Used with permission.
13, "Exchange Student Makes Lifelong Impression," by Elizabeth Atcheson. Reprinted courtesy of the *Tuscaloosa News,* Tuscaloosa, Alabama, April 12, 1994, p. 8A.
14 (also tape and tapescript), "From Government Official to Immigrant," by an Afghan immigrant as interviewed by Janet Robinson. Used with permission.
15–16, "That's What I Want to Be," by JoAn D. Criddle. *Bamboo & Butterflies: From Refugee to Citizen.* Dixon, Calif.: East/West BRIDGE Publishing House, 1992, pp. 79–83. Used with permission.
18–19, "Steps in Cultural Understanding" contains some concepts selected from Robert G. Hanvey, "Cross-Cultural Awareness," in Louise F. Luce, ed., *The Spanish-Speaking World: An Anthology of Cross-Cultural Perspectives,* Lincolnwood, Ill.: National Textbook Co., 1992, p. 22ff.; and Jan Gaston, *Cross-Cultural Awareness Teaching Techniques,* Brattleboro, Vt.: ProLingua Associates, 1984.
22–23, "Typical Americans" from *Typical American.* Copyright © 1991 by Gish Jen. Reprinted by permission of Houghton Mifflin Co. All rights reserved.
24 (also tape and tapescript), "Stereotypes Everywhere," by Hans Kaufman as interviewed by Catherine L. Callender. Used with permission.
27 (also tape and tapescript), "My Experiences with Culture Shock," by Young Ye Park-Oh. Used with permission.
37–38, "Monochronic Time (M-Time) and Polychronic Time (P-Time)," by Edward T. Hall and Mildred Reed Hall. Understanding Cultural Differences, reprinted with permission of Intercultural Press, Inc., Yarmouth, Me. Copyright © 1990, pp. 13–15.
40 (also tape and tapescript), "More About M-Time and P-Time." John Condon, *Good Neighbors: Communicating with the Mexicans,* reprinted with permission of Intercultural Press, Inc., Yarmouth, Me. Copyright © 1985, pp. 65–66.
44, "Keeping Time," by Betty L. as interviewed by Rebecca L. Oxford. Used with permission.
45, "I Know My Priorities," by Jorge V. as interviewed by Rebecca L. Oxford. Used with permission.
48, "A Science Fiction View of Time and Space" from *Sideshow* by Sheri S. Tepper. Copyright © 1993. Used by permission of Bantam Books, a division of Bantam Doubleday Dell Publishing Group, Inc.
49, "A Scientific View of Time and Space," by Edward T. Hall and Mildred Reed Hall. *Understanding Cultural Differences,* reprinted with permission of Intercultural Press, Inc., Yarmouth, Me. Copyright © 1990, pp. 15–16.
50 (also tape and tapescript), "Territory and Personal Space," by Edward T. Hall and Mildred Reed Hall. *Understanding Cultural Differences,* reprinted with permission of Intercultural Press, Inc., Yarmouth, Me. Copyright © 1990, pp. 10–12.
52, "Other Kinds of Space in North American Culture: Intimate, Social, and Public." From *Body Language.* Copyright © 1970 by Julius Fast, pp. 30–34 (slightly adapted). Reprinted by permission of the publisher, M. Evans and Company, Inc.

55–56, "Sacred Space in Germany and Other Northern European Countries" contains some concepts from John C. Condon and Fathi Yousef, "Out of House and Home," in Louise F. Luce and Elise C. Smith (eds.), *Toward Internationalism: Readings in Cross-Cultural Communication,* pp. 99–116, Cambridge, Mass.: Newbury House/Harper & Row, 1977; and also from Nancy L. Braganti and Elizabeth Devine, *European Customs and Manners,* New York: Simon & Schuster, 1992.
59, "My Son and I Discover Latin Space," by Maury M. Breecher. Used with permission.
60 (also tape and tapescript), "Space in Japan and Some Arabic-Speaking Countries." From *Body Language.* Copyright © 1970 by Julius Fast (slightly adapted). Reprinted by permission of the publisher, M. Evans and Company, Inc.
70 (also tape and tapescript), "Please Touch (Sometimes)," by Roger Axtell, from *Do's and Taboos Around the World.* 3rd ed. New York: John Wiley, 1993, pp. 43–44 (slightly adapted). Used with permission.
71, "Should I Touch or Not?" contains some concepts adapted from *Culturgrams,* Provo, Utah: Brigham Young University, 1992.
77 (also tape and tapescript), "Risky Body Language," by Roger Axtell, from *Do's and Taboos Around the World.* 3rd ed. New York: John Wiley, 1993, pp. 43–44 (slightly adapted). Used with permission.
78, "Universal and Culture-Specific Gestures" contains some concepts adapted from Genelle Morain, "Kinesics and Cross-Cultural Understanding," in Louise F. Luce and Elise C. Smith (eds.), *Toward Internationalism Readings in Cross-Cultural Communication.* Cambridge, Mass: Newbury House/Harper & Row, pp. 117–142.
84 (also tape and tapescript), "Other Gestures" contains some concepts adapted from *Culturgrams.* Provo, Utah: Brigham Young University, 1992.
88 (also tape and tapescript), "I Slouched My Way to a Cross-Cultural Insult," by Bob Tripp. Used with permission.
90, "Eye Language," by Roger Axtell, from *Do's and Taboos Around the World.* 3rd ed. New York: John Wiley, p. 42. Used with permission.
93, "The Story of Livia," from *Body Language*. Copyright © 1970 by Julius Fast. Reprinted by permission of the publisher, M. Evans and Company, Inc.
94 (also tape and tapescript), "Double Face," by Amy Tan, excerpted from *The Joy Luck Club*, New York: G.P. Putnam's Sons, 1989, pp. 254–256. Used with permission.
108 (also tape and tapescript),"The Supreme Importance of Families: Contrasts Between North Americans and Mexicans." John Condon, *Good Neighbors: Communicating with the Mexicans,* reprinted with permission of Intercultural Press, Inc., Yarmouth, Me. Copyright © 1985, pp. 23–25.
110, "I Want My Parents to Be Proud of Me," by John L. as interviewed by Leah Zuch. Used with permission.
111 (also tape and tapescript), "Three Generations of Single Mothers," by Michelle Ingrassia. From *Newsweek*, Aug. 30, 1993, p. 25, and copyright © 1993, Newsweek, Inc. All rights reserved. Reprinted by permission.
112, "Father Oriented Toward Cuba, Son Toward America," by David Rieff, *The Exile: Cuba in the Heart of Miami.* New York: Wylie, Aitken, & Stone, 1993. Used with permission.
113 (also tape and tapescript), "The Child Bearers," *45 Mercy Street* by Anne Sexton. Copyright © 1976 by Linda Gray Sexton and Loring Conant, Jr. Reprinted by permission of Houghton Mifflin Co. All rights reserved.
113 (also tape and tapescript), "Point Sur," *Doublespace,* pp. 81–82. Copyright © 1992 by Hank Lazer. Reprinted by permission of the Segue Foundation, New York.
115, "A Special Kind of Mother," by Banana Yoshimoto, translated by Megan Backus, pp. 11–14, 41–42. Copyright © 1993 by Megan Backus, © 1988 by Banana Yoshimoto. Used by permission of Grove/Atlantic, Inc.
116 (also tape and tapescript), "Choosing Mates" contains some concepts adapted from William Kornblum, *Sociology in a Changing World,* New York: Holt, Rinehart and Winston, 1988.
117, "Habitation" from *Procedures for Underground* by Margaret Atwood. Copyright © Oxford University Press Canada, 1970. Reprinted by permission of Oxford University Press.
118 (also tape and tapescript), "Friend Maria Elena and I Have Different Views About Divorce," by Michael Chrismartin. Used with permission.
120–121, "The Worst Kind of Abuse," by Sylvia F. Used with permission.
122, "Battle of the Sexes Continues," by Roger Axtell, from *Do's and Taboos Around the World.* 3rd ed. New York: John Wiley, pp. 22–25. Used with permission.
123, "Female Oppression," by Mary Livermore, Lecture, 1867. Public domain.
124, "Reducing Women to Their Correct Status," by Suzette Haden Elgin. *The Judas Rose: Native Tongue II.* New York: DAW Books, Inc., 1987, pp. 49–50. Used with permission.
125, "Running the Show, Pressing the Buttons, Making the Money," by Ursula Le Guin, Bryn Mawr College Commencement Address, 1986, in *Dancing at the Edge of the World: Thoughts on Words, Women, Places.* Copyright © 1989 Grove/Atlantic, Inc., pp. 147–190. Used with permission.
128, "When Violence Hits Home," by U.S. Rep. Dan Burton in *People Weekly,* April 4, 1994, pp. 91–96. Reprinted by permission of *People Weekly.*
132 (also tape and tapescript), "Top Seven Problems in Schools" and "Three Things Children Need." From *Familyhood,* pp. 38–39 and 190. Copyright © Lee Salk, 1992. Reprinted by permission of Authors & Artists Group, Inc.
132 (also tape and tapescript), "Tips for a Happy Marriage." From *Delicious! Your Magazine for Natural Living,* May/June, 1993, p. 35. Reprinted by permission of New Hope Communications, Inc.

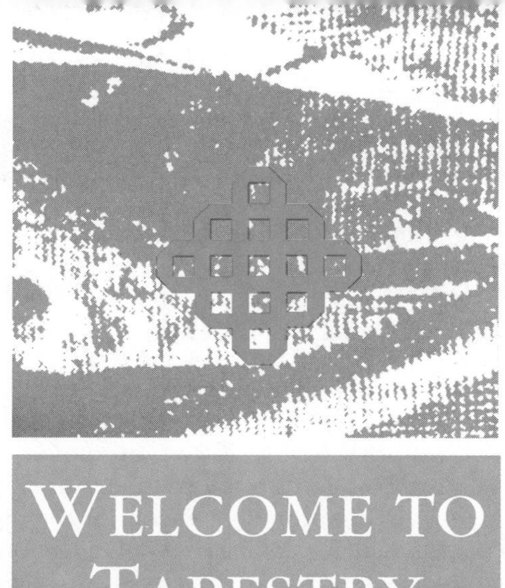

Welcome to Tapestry

Enter the world of Tapestry! Language learning can be seen as an ever-developing tapestry woven with many threads and colors. The elements of the tapestry are related to different language skills like listening and speaking, reading and writing; the characteristics of the teachers; the desires, needs, and backgrounds of the students; and the general second language development process. When all these elements are working together harmoniously, the result is a colorful, continuously growing tapestry of language competence of which the student and the teacher can be proud.

This volume is part of the Tapestry Program for students of English as a second language (ESL) at levels from beginning to "bridge" (which follows the advanced level and prepares students to enter regular postsecondary programs along with native English speakers). Tapestry levels include:

Beginning
Low Intermediate
High Intermediate
Advanced
High Advanced
Bridge

Because the Tapestry Program provides a unified theoretical and pedagogical foundation for all its components, you can optimally use all the Tapestry student books in a coordinated fashion as an entire curriculum of materials. (They will be published from 1993 to 1995 with further editions likely thereafter.) Alternatively, you can decide to use just certain Tapestry volumes, depending on your specific needs.

Tapestry is primarily designed for ESL students at postsecondary institutions in North America. Some want to learn ESL for academic or career advancement, others for social and personal reasons. Tapestry builds directly on all these motivations. Tapestry stimulates learners to do their best. It enables learners to use English naturally and to develop fluency as well as accuracy.

Tapestry Principles

The following principles underlie the instruction provided in all of the components of the Tapestry Program.

EMPOWERING LEARNERS

Language learners in Tapestry classrooms are active and increasingly responsible for developing their English language skills and related cultural abilities. This self direction leads to better, more rapid learning. Some cultures virtually train their students to be passive in the classroom, but Tapestry weans them from passivity by providing exceptionally high interest materials, colorful and motivating activities, personalized self-reflection tasks, peer tutoring and other forms of cooperative learning, and powerful learning strategies to boost self direction in learning.

The empowerment of learners creates refreshing new roles for teachers, too. The teacher serves as facilitator, co-communicator, diagnostician, guide, and helper. Teachers are set free to be more creative at the same time their students become more autonomous learners.

HELPING STUDENTS IMPROVE THEIR LEARNING STRATEGIES

Learning strategies are the behaviors or steps an individual uses to enhance his or her learning. Examples are taking notes, practicing, finding a conversation partner, analyzing words, using background knowledge, and controlling anxiety. Hundreds of such strategies have been identified. Successful language learners use language learning strategies that are most effective for them given their particular learning style, and they put them together smoothly to fit the needs of a given language task. On the other hand, the learning strategies of less successful learners are a desperate grab-bag of ill-matched techniques.

All learners need to know a wide range of learning strategies. All learners need systematic practice in choosing and applying strategies that are relevant for various learning needs. Tapestry is one of the only ESL programs that overtly weaves a comprehensive set of learning strategies into language activities in all its volumes. These learning strategies are arranged in six broad categories throughout the Tapestry books:

Forming concepts
Personalizing
Remembering new material
Managing your learning
Understanding and using emotions
Overcoming limitations

The most useful strategies are sometimes repeated and flagged with a note, "It Works! Learning Strategy . . ." to remind students to use a learning strategy they have already encountered. This recycling reinforces the value of learning strategies and provides greater practice.

RECOGNIZING AND HANDLING LEARNING STYLES EFFECTIVELY

Learners have different learning styles (for instance, visual, auditory, hands-on; reflective, impulsive; analytic, global; extroverted, introverted; closure-oriented, open). Particularly in an ESL setting, where students come from vastly different cultural backgrounds, learning styles differences abound and can cause "style conflicts."

Unlike most language instruction materials, Tapestry provides exciting activities specifically tailored to the needs of students with a large range of learning styles. You can use any Tapestry volume with the confidence that the activities and materials are intentionally geared for many different styles. Insights from the latest educational and psychological research undergird this style-nourishing variety.

OFFERING AUTHENTIC, MEANINGFUL COMMUNICATION

Students need to encounter language that provides authentic, meaningful communication. They must be involved in real-life communication tasks that cause them to *want* and *need* to read, write, speak, and listen to English. Moreover, the tasks—to be most effective—must be arranged around themes relevant to learners.

Themes like family relationships, survival in the educational system, personal health, friendships in a new country, political changes, and protection of the environment are all valuable to ESL learners. Tapestry focuses on topics like these. In every Tapestry volume, you will see specific content drawn from very broad areas such as home life, science and technology, business, humanities, social sciences, global issues, and multiculturalism. All the themes are real and important, and they are fashioned into language tasks that students enjoy.

At the advanced level, Tapestry also includes special books each focused on a single broad theme. For instance, there are two books on business English, two on English for science and technology, and two on academic communication and study skills.

UNDERSTANDING AND VALUING DIFFERENT CULTURES

Many ESL books and programs focus completely on the "new" culture, that is, the culture which the students are entering. The implicit message is that ESL students should just learn about this target culture, and there is no need to understand their own culture better or to find out about the cultures of their international classmates. To some ESL students, this makes them feel their own culture is not valued in the new country.

Tapestry is designed to provide a clear and understandable entry into North American culture. Nevertheless, the Tapestry Program values *all* the cultures found in the ESL classroom. Tapestry students have constant opportunities to become "culturally fluent" in North American culture while they are learning English, but they also have the chance to think about the cultures of their classmates and even understand their home culture from different perspectives.

INTEGRATING THE LANGUAGE SKILLS

Communication in a language is not restricted to one skill or another. ESL students are typically expected to learn (to a greater or lesser degree) all four language skills: reading, writing, speaking. and listening. They are also expected to develop strong grammatical competence, as well as becoming socioculturally sensitive and knowing what to do when they encounter a "language barrier."

Research shows that multi-skill learning is more effective than isolated-skill learning, because related activities in several skills provide reinforcement and refresh the learner's memory. Therefore, Tapestry integrates all the skills. A given Tapestry volume might highlight one skill, such as reading, but all other skills are also included to support and strengthen overall language development.

However, many intensive ESL programs are divided into classes labeled according to one skill (Reading Comprehension Class) or at most two skills (Listening/Speaking Class or Oral Communication Class). The volumes in the Tapestry Program can easily be used to fit this traditional format, because each volume clearly identifies its highlighted or central skill(s).

Grammar is interwoven into all Tapestry volumes. However, there is also a separate reference book for students, *The Tapestry Grammar,* and a Grammar Strand composed of grammar "work-out" books at each of the levels in the Tapestry Program.

Other Features of the Tapestry Program

PILOT SITES

It is not enough to provide volumes full of appealing tasks and beautiful pictures. Users deserve to know that the materials have been pilot-tested. In many ESL series, pilot testing takes place at only a few sites or even just in the classroom of the author. In contrast, Heinle & Heinle Publishers have developed a network of Tapestry Pilot Test Sites throughout North America. At this time, there are approximately 40 such sites, although the number grows weekly. These sites try out the materials and provide suggestions for revisions. They are all actively engaged in making Tapestry the best program possible.

AN OVERALL GUIDEBOOK

To offer coherence to the entire Tapestry Program and especially to offer support for teachers who want to understand the principles and practice of Tapestry, we have written a book entitled, *The Tapestry of Language Learning. The Individual in the Communicative Classroom* (Scarcella and Oxford, published in 1992 by Heinle & Heinle).

A Last Word

We are pleased to welcome you to Tapestry! We use the Tapestry principles every day, and we hope these principles—and all the books in the Tapestry Program—provide you the same strength, confidence, and joy that they give us. We look forward to comments from both teachers and students who use any part of the Tapestry Program.

Rebecca L. Oxford
University of Alabama
Tuscaloosa, Alabama

Robin C. Scarcella
University of California at Irvine
Irvine, California

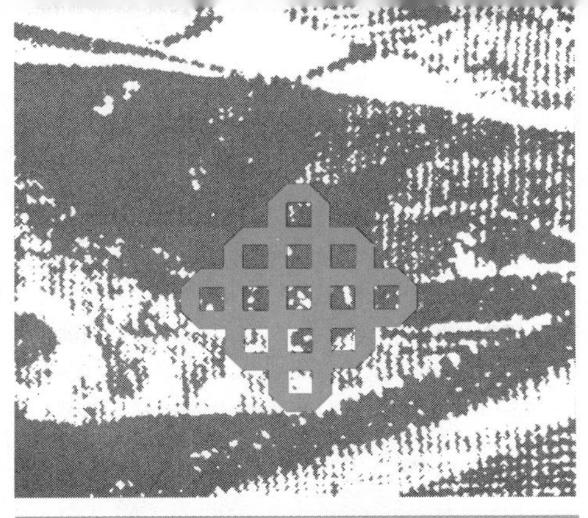

PREFACE

Patterns in This Book

Every human act—tipping your head, lowering or raising your eyes, smiling at someone you love, whispering a prayer, revving up a motorcycle, combing your hair in a certain way, greeting your friend, chatting with your family, accepting a suggestion from your boss or your teacher, exchanging money and goods at the market—is a cultural act. Culture is the dance of life of all humanity.

Culture is the loom, weaving the patterns of our lives. "We sleep, but the loom of life never stops, and the pattern which was weaving when the sun went down is weaving when it comes up tomorrow," said writer Henry Ward Beecher.

Culture is the human face of mercy and the bloody act of war. Culture is anguished people praying for help and happy people laughing for joy. Culture is the shoulder against the plow, the arm carrying the water bucket, the hand with the baton leading the symphony. Culture is the sweetness of love and touch. Culture is also the bitter taste of hatred. Tom Scovel, specialist on language and culture, describes culture as "the social cement of all human relationships."

In this book you will see many cultural patterns. Chapter 1 is a general introduction to patterns of culture. Time and space are explored in Chapter 2. Chapter 3 deals with physical aspects of culture: touch, gesture, posture, and gaze (the language of the eyes). In Chapter 4 are family patterns, including among others marriage, children, home violence, and gender roles. The Afterword shows how new cultural patterns can emerge.

Some important cultural patterns are not *directly* treated in this book because of lack of space. Among these key themes are religion, information sharing, styles of teaching and learning, and concepts of life and death. These require another book! Yet no doubt these patterns have *indirectly* crept into the chapters of this book. These patterns, in one way or another, can influence how people view cultures, handle time and space, move their bodies, and act within their families.

This book uses an international, multicultural approach. This approach highlights North American culture while also honoring—through stories and examples—many cultures from all over the world. Stories of real people, spoken in their own words, demonstrate different cultural patterns and show how individuals interact with culture.

To help you communicate about culture, this book integrates all four language skills (reading, writing, speaking, and listening) in a variety of culture-and-language tasks. Every chapter offers you "learning strategies," steps you can take to make your own learning easier.

Putting this all together, your three goals in this book are:

- to expand your understanding of culture
- to improve your English communication skills
- to strengthen your learning ability through learning strategies

Acknowledgments

I have many people to thank for their help regarding this book. First and foremost I want to thank Linda Ward Burgess, who read the original manuscript (every word!) and shared her deep cultural insights with me. She also suggested that I consider including her multicultural-education graduate students' interviews of people who had experienced different cultures. Indeed, these interviews proved to be a fascinating and wonderful addition to the book. Each of the interviews showed courage, determination, and a great effort to understand the new culture. I want to express my heartfelt gratitude to the interviewers and interviewees for allowing me to include their work in this book:

- Janet Robinson, who interviewed an Afghan immigrant
- Catherine L. Callender, who interviewed Hans Kaufman
- Leah Zuch, who interviewed John L.

It is my pleasure to thank Amy Jamison, my developmental editor, for her patience, good ideas, and synthesizing ability. Thanks, too, to Marta Dmytrenko-Ahrabian, Wayne State University; Pamela Flash, University of Minnesota; Janet Jalloul, Miami-Dade Community College; Bessie Karras-Lazarus, California State University, Northridge; and Laura LeDréan, University of Houston–Downtown. Those brave reviewers gave me helpful hints and must be thanked for their eager willingness to trudge through the 15 initial chapters.

My husband, Maury Breecher, was a dear and helpful critic at every stage of this book. In addition, professional assistance consistently came from Dr. Young Ye Park-Oh, my former graduate student, from Amany Saleh, doctoral candidate, and from Jennifer Drawhorn, master's candidate, all from the University of Alabama. I give my most loving thanks to all four: Maury, Young, Amany, and Jennifer.

Of course, Dave Lee and Ken Mattsson of Heinle & Heinle Publishers were my constant companions on this cultural trek—as they have been throughout the birth and life of the Tapestry Program. They nudged, encouraged, and aided. They have both been a major positive force in my life as colleagues and friends. Thanks to the fine support of Heinle & Heinle Publishers, particularly Charles Heinle and

Stanley Galek, who recognized the Tapestry Program as something that could be greatly valuable for our field. I also want to thank Robin Scarcella, my Tapestry co-editor, for her inspiration. She taught me a great deal about cross-culturalism by her example and through her writings. Deepest appreciation goes to Elaine Hall at PC&F for her masterful production work.

Rebecca L. Oxford, Ph.D.
Professor, University of Alabama
Tuscaloosa, Alabama

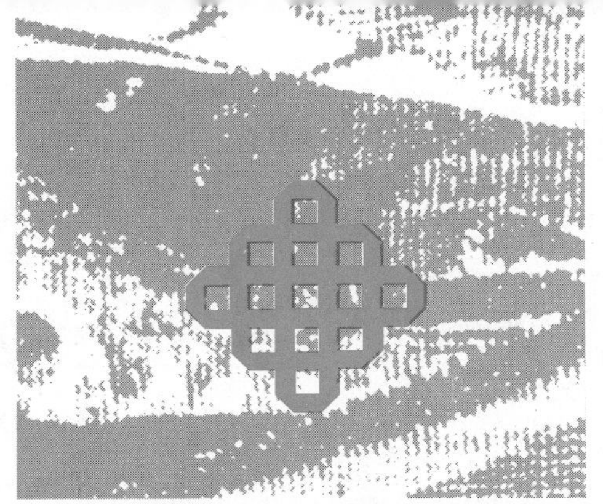

Contents

1 CHAPTER

Patterns of Culture

INTRODUCTION

PREVIEW QUESTIONS

1. What are the differences between "everyday" culture and "**sophisticated**"* culture?
2. What lies beneath the surface of the iceberg of culture?
3. How do personal experiences of a new culture differ?
4. How can a person's cultural understanding change over time?
5. What are two different views of culture shock?

I too am a rare
Pattern.

—Amy Lowell

PATTERNS IN THIS CHAPTER

This chapter introduces you to different cultural patterns: culture as "everyday" life vs. "sophisticated" cultural activities and attitudes, and culture as an **iceberg.** In this pattern you will find information about the growth of cultural understanding and about culture shock. This chapter also shares stories of people who have learned to live in a new culture. Each pattern holds its own special meaning for you as a learner of English. You will probably relate to some patterns better than to others. Try to learn from all of them!

Culture wears many different guises.

*Words in text set in bold type are listed alphabetically and defined in the Word Patterns section on pages 28–29 of this chapter.

YOUR SUCCESS PATTERNS IN THIS CHAPTER

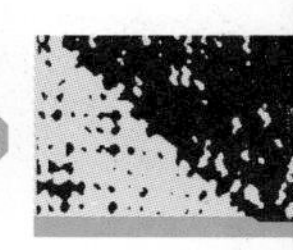

By the end of this chapter, you will be able to:

- describe the differences between "everyday" and "sophisticated" culture;
- identify the parts of the cultural iceberg;
- consider the steps in cultural understanding;
- describe two different views of culture shock;
- analyze several people's experiences of life in a new culture; and
- use many new learning strategies to make your studying easier.

Threads

We are confronted by insurmountable opportunities.

Pogo

LEARNING STRATEGY

Managing Your Learning: Assessing your own abilities helps you know what you need to learn.

Task 1.1 Evaluating

THINKING ABOUT YOURSELF

Step 1. Assess your current ability by circling the actions above that you can do *now.*

Step 2. Which actions did you *not* circle? These are the actions to which you can pay most attention in this chapter. (If you did not circle any, then this chapter can be significant in boosting your cultural growth.)

Step 3. In your notebook, list three reasons why you would like to understand culture better.

Step 4. Discuss your reasons with at least one other person. Are your reasons the same or different?

CULTURAL PATTERN 1: ASPECTS OF CULTURE

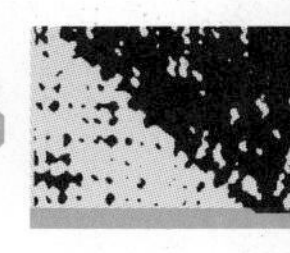

LEARNING STRATEGY

Forming Concepts: Brainstorming—quickly generating ideas with other people and writing the ideas down without criticizing or organizing them—is a great way to build your understanding.

Task 1.2 Prereading

BRAINSTORMING CULTURE

By yourself or with others, brainstorm all the words and ideas that you think about when you consider the word "culture." Write them in your notebook.

LEARNING STRATEGY

Overcoming Limitations: Guessing meanings from the context helps you get the idea quickly and strengthen your knowledge.

Task 1.3 Reading

GUESSING AS YOU READ

As you read, guess the meanings of words you do not know from the other words in the sentence or the paragraph. The context around a word often helps!

Everyday culture and sophisticated culture

Culture includes everyday behavior and attitudes. It involves how people live each day, what they do, and what patterns of living and rules they follow. This part of culture is sometimes called "everyday" culture. It includes:

- where people go
- what they make and grow
- what they eat
- what they wear for daily life
- what they say at different times
- what they say to different people
- what kinds of work they do
- how they play
- how they use time
- how they deal with conflict
- how they buy and sell, and
- what and how they learn
- what they believe
- how they worship
- whom they honor and trust
- what or whom they hate
- what is saddening
- what is joyful
- what is **repugnant**
- what is funny or **entertaining**
- what they will fight for
- how they organize groups.

A different way to look at culture is as personal **refinement** or **sophistication.** This might be called "sophisticated" culture. If you write fine music or create great art, you are contributing a form of culture to the rest of humanity. If you notice the beautiful lines of an old church or **mosque,** you are appreciating culture. When you enjoy fine symphonies, paintings, or sculptures, you are participating in culture.

Remember that just because the terms "everyday" and "sophisticated" might be used, that doesn't mean one is *better* than the other. They both add to the overall culture.

Some everyday cultural patterns, such as daily prejudice, might be negative, while others, such as everyday kindness, might be positive. Some patterns of sophisticated culture, like **intricately** designed torture halls, might be negative, while others, like magnificent paintings, might be positive. All these are parts of the total picture of culture.

Task 1.4 Postreading

CHECKING YOUR COMPREHENSION

Complete these steps based on the reading above.

Step 1. Jot down all the examples you have found (in the readings or elsewhere) for the following:
- everyday culture
- sophisticated culture

Step 2. Which of these two (everyday culture or sophisticated culture) more clearly represents the central core of a culture, in your opinion? Write your answer in your notebook, and write at least two reasons.

Step 3. Compare and discuss your comments with those of someone else.

Threads

There are only two or three human stories, and they go on repeating themselves as fiercely as if they had never happened before.

Novelist Willa Cather

Task 1.5 Expanding Your Knowledge

CONSIDERING YOUR FAVORITE CULTURAL THEMES OR TOPICS

LEARNING STRATEGY

Remembering New Material: Listing cultural topics helps you remember them and also expands your understanding.

Step 1. What are some interesting cultural themes or topics you would like to explore? List as many as you can in your notebook.

Step 2. Discuss your list with someone else. Whose is longer and more detailed? Do you want to expand yours any further at this time? If so, do it right now.

LEARNING STRATEGY

Forming Concepts: Making a concept map helps you understand ideas more rapidly and more easily.

Task 1.6 Expanding Your Knowledge

CREATING A CONCEPT MAP OF CULTURE

Using all the examples in this chapter so far, create a concept map of culture.

Step 1. Understand the meaning of a "concept map." A concept map is simply a set of related concepts or ideas laid out on a piece of paper. The concepts are connected by lines or arrows to show which concepts are most strongly related.

Step 2. Put the concept CULTURE in the center of the map, as shown in the example at the top of page 7.

Step 3. Add concepts all around the central concept, CULTURE. For instance, you might add RELIGION, FAMILIES, SCHOOLS, COOKING, EATING, WORKING, and so on.

Step 4. Link all these with the main idea using lines or arrows.

Step 5. Break down all these concepts into smaller parts. For instance, RELIGION might divide into CHURCH, TEMPLE, SHRINE, BUDDHA, and so on. Link these smaller parts with the larger ones with lines or arrows.

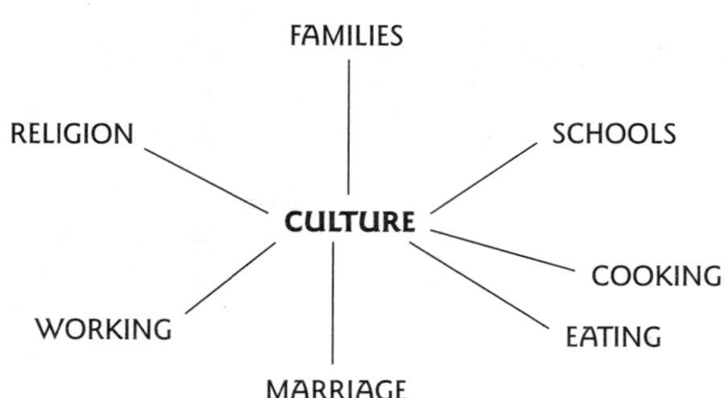

Example of a concept map of culture.

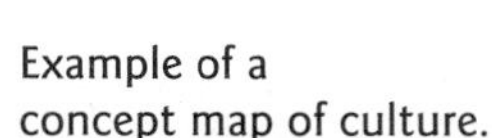

Step 6. Compare your concept map with the map(s) of one or two other people. Expand your map in any way you want. Make it as **comprehensive** as possible.

Step 7. As you learn more about culture in later chapters, you can add even more concepts to your concept map.

Task 1.7 Expanding Your Knowledge

INTRODUCING YOURSELF TO ANOTHER CULTURE

Do one or more of the following steps:

Step 1. In a group of three to five people, each person first introduces himself or herself by means of a significant incident that happened to him or her illustrating some aspect of the person's native culture.

Step 2. Each person introduces himself or herself in his or her native language, just as would be done in the home culture, and then provides a direct translation into English.

Step 3. Each person introduces himself or herself to the group nonverbally (through signs, gestures, drawings, etc.).

Step 4. Each person gives his or her name and one important thing about himself or herself.

Step 5. Each person introduces another member of the group from a different culture after five minutes of "interviewing time."

Threads

Mind is actually internalized culture.

Edward T. Hall

Source: Task 1.7 contains some concepts adapted from Robert Moran. In William H. Weeks, Paul B. Pedersen, and Richard W. Brislin, eds., *A Manual of Structured Experiences for Cross-Cultural Learning.* Yarmouth, Me.: Intercultural Press, 1990.

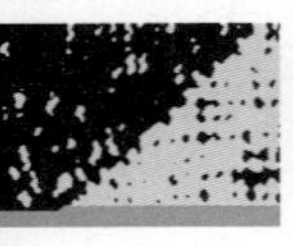

CULTURAL PATTERN 2: THE ICEBERG OF CULTURE

Task 1.8 Prelistening

Threads

The unexamined life is not worth living.

Socrates

CONSIDERING THE ICEBERG

Step 1. Take a look at the picture of the iceberg.
Step 2. Discuss with others:
- **a.** How much of the iceberg is covered by water?
- **b.** How much remains above the surface for people to see?
- **c.** How does this relate to culture?

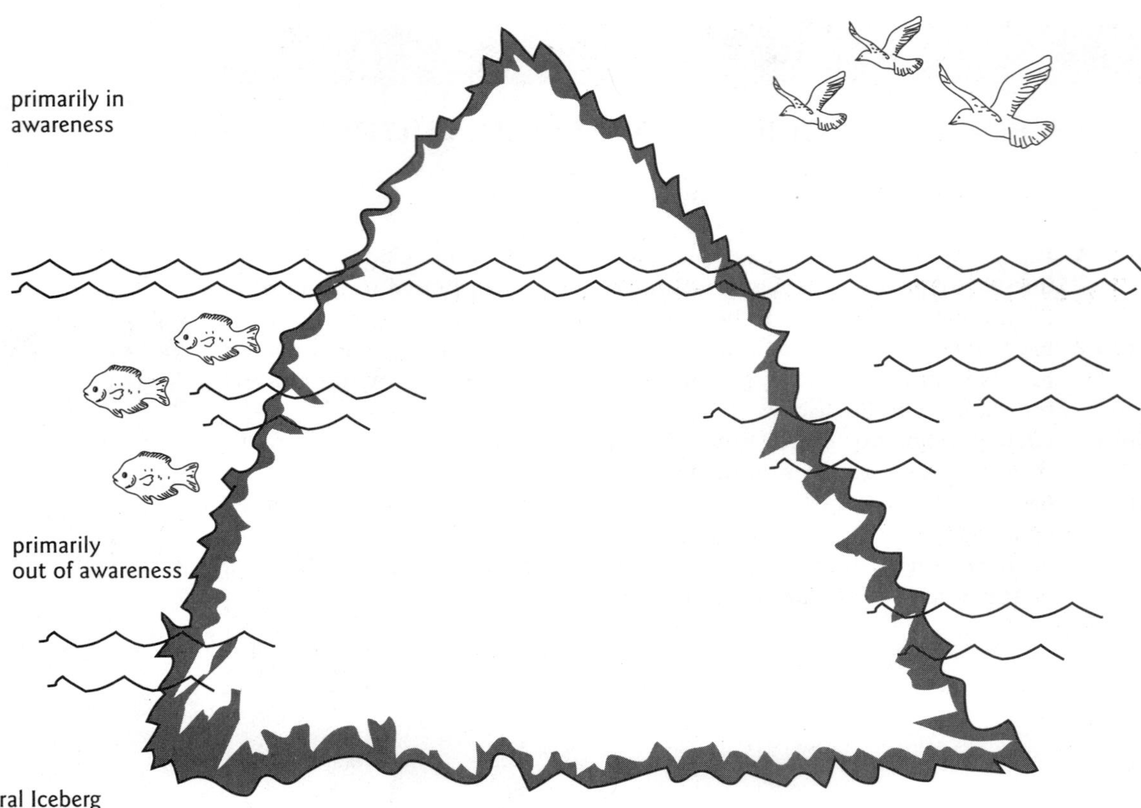

The Cultural Iceberg

LEARNING STRATEGY

Forming Concepts: Completing a drawing and then discussing it can sometimes clarify an important cultural concept.

Task 1.9 Listening

COMPLETING THE ICEBERG DRAWING

As you listen to the passage, write on the iceberg drawing the cultural aspects that are *above the water line* and the cultural aspects that are *below the water line.* Label all the parts of the iceberg that you can, according to the guidelines of the speaker.

Your tape has **"The Cultural Iceberg,"** which contains some concepts adapted from Edward T. Hall, *The Hidden Dimension.* Garden City, New York: Anchor Books, 1969.

Task 1.10 Postlistening

CHECKING YOUR LABELS

Step 1. Check to see whether your labels are correct. (You may listen to the tape again if necessary.)
Step 2. Correct the placement of any labels that are misplaced.
Step 3. Add to the cultural iceberg picture anything you missed the first time around.
Step 4. Compare your drawing with that of someone else and discuss any differences.

Task 1.11 Expanding Your Knowledge

PLACING THE ASPECTS OF CULTURE WHERE THEY BELONG

Step 1. At right are 20 additional aspects of culture we haven't talked about. Make sure you understand the meaning of each one.
Step 2. Cut 20 strips of paper.
Step 3. Copy the names of cultural aspects onto the strips of paper.
Step 4. Place these strips above or below the water line on the iceberg—the line of awareness—where you believe they belong.
Step 5. Compare your arrangement with that of somebody else. What are the differences? Do these differences make sense? Go back to the listening passage and recheck your understanding. Do you want to change anything about your iceberg now, or do you want to keep it as it is?

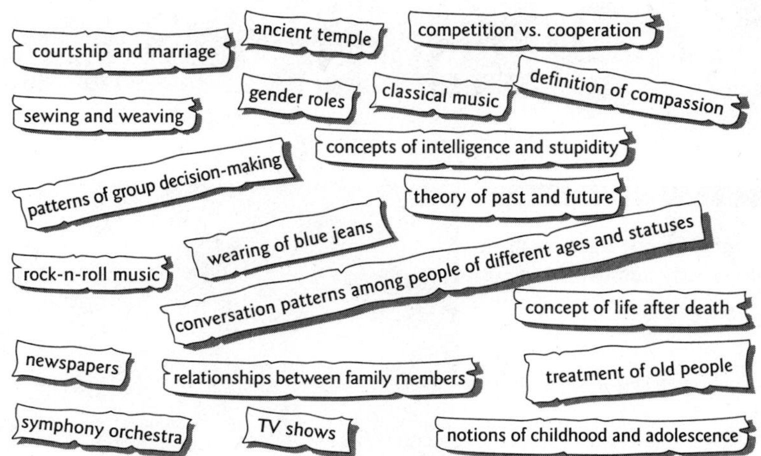

Task 1.12 Expanding Your Knowledge

FINDING CULTURAL OBJECTS

Step 1. A person from the new culture writes up short lists, one list for each pair of participants (or group of three). Each list contains five items (objects, artifacts) to be found in your new culture. All the lists are different. These items might be **nonprescription** medicines, cosmetics, decorations, food, household supplies, religious tokens, musical tapes, recreational objects, office items, and so on. Each object reflects the culture.

Some cultural objects you might find

Step 2. Work in pairs or groups of three to find the objects on your lists. Learn as much as you can about how the objects are used so you can explain or demonstrate the use later. You will have three hours.

Step 3. Come back three hours after you have begun Step 2. Show each item on the list, and demonstrate and explain its use. (You can bring along a demonstrator from the native culture for Step 3.) Watch and listen as other people share what was on their lists.

Step 4. Describe any interesting experiences involved in Steps 1–3.

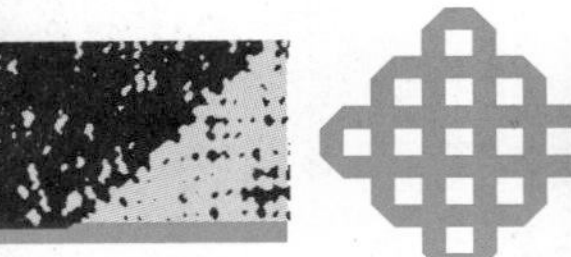

CULTURAL PATTERN 3: ADJUSTING TO AMERICAN CULTURE

Ashraf is on the right, with wife Amany and daughter Mariam.

Task 1.13 Prelistening

ANALYZING NAMES

Given the names of Ashraf and Sayed, which part of the world do you think these people are from? What problems might people from that part of the world have with U.S. culture? Why? What might they miss from their own culture?

LEARNING STRATEGY

Forming Concepts: Using a T-line to take notes helps you understand more fully.

Task 1.14 Listening

USING THE T-LINE

As you listen, take notes using a T-line as shown below. On the left side, take notes on how Ashraf deals with U.S. culture, and on the right side, take notes on how Sayed handles it.

Your tape has "**Ashraf and Sayed Deal with U.S. Culture,**" by Ashraf el Sayed. Used with permission.

DEALING WITH U.S. CULTURE

HOW ASHRAF DID IT	HOW SAYED DID IT

LEARNING STRATEGY

Understanding and Using Emotions: Examining the feelings of other people can help you understand and get along with those people more easily.

Task 1.15 Postlistening

UNDERSTANDING FEELINGS AND NEEDS

Step 1. In your notebook, list things Ashraf did to feel more comfortable in the U.S. culture.
Step 2. Explain in your notebook why Sayed felt so lonely and sad.
Step 3. Write what Ashraf did to help Sayed and what Sayed did to help himself.
Step 4. Is it typical for people to feel as upset and sad as Sayed did when he arrived? Why or why not?
Step 5. Discuss your answers with a small group. Note differences and similarities. Are there any cultural influences on these differences and similarities?

Task 1.16 Prereading

CONSIDERING THE IMPACT OF EXCHANGE STUDENTS

Discuss with other people: What is an "exchange student"? How long does an exchange student usually stay? Does an exchange student typically visit many families or just one? How would having an exchange student in your house affect your family?

Task 1.17 Reading

LOOKING FOR THE EFFECTS

As you read the story, make a list of the effects of Kathy, the exchange student, on Elizabeth, her family, and her community.

Exchange student leaves a lifelong impression

by Elizabeth Atcheson

Love in any language,
Straight from the heart
Pulls us all together
And never apart
And once we learn to speak it,
All the world will hear.

—Sandi Patti,
"Love in Any Language"

Sandi Patti, a popular contemporary Christian vocalist, sang that song a few years ago. It was Kathy, however, who made the song real to me.

Katharina Gabriella Rutzler was her full German name, but my Southern family shortened her name to "Kathy" almost immediately after her arrival.

As an exchange student who lived with my family for 10 months, Kathy taught us that even though we don't speak the same language or perhaps accept the same ideals, we can still love each other.

She arrived in August 1989 and our family immediately loved her. Many times, she reminded us of how fortunate we are to live in the United States.

Since Kathy lived within miles of the wall separating [the former] East and West Germany, she told us stories of how she had lain in bed at night listening to gunshots as people attempted to escape the Communist East Berlin.

She loved the way America was so spacious and open, and she envied the fact that most of us live in houses rather than apartments like the crowded ones so common in her country. She especially enjoyed Southern hospitality, Alabama football, cookouts, and cornbread.

Because Kathy was so outgoing, she quickly made friends at Central High School—East Campus, where she was a senior. She received the highest grade in both her English and Latin classes. She regularly attended Friday night football games and slumber parties. She played on the school tennis team and was involved in our church.

Elizabeth

She even received an invitation to her senior prom.

Certainly she was experiencing all the joys of high school in America, **relishing** each activity. She even went through graduation with the 1990 senior class.

Although many exciting things happened in Kathy's life that year, perhaps the most significant was the fall of Communism in Germany. From our family room, she watched on television as many of her friends danced on the historic wall in celebration. Kathy was ecstatic.

Many of her friends sent her pieces of the wall. She was overjoyed when her mother reminded her that she would never have to listen to gunshots at night again. Everyone was finally free.

Decidedly, our family taught Kathy many things. My father and mother taught her to drive on Sunday afternoons at the Coleman Coliseum parking lot. We taught her the rules of football, and she went to the Sugar Bowl with our family. We also taught her how to budget her money.

Kathy was my friend and my sister, and that is exactly what she wanted to be. Kathy longed to be a part of our family, and sure enough, she became like family to us. Frequently, she would prepare German meals for us so that we would be more familiar with her culture.

Kathy added so much to our family. We just couldn't believe that a person [from] thousands of miles away could so easily fit into our home life.

She left the United States in June 1990. Things were quiet at my house for awhile. It was a sad time for my younger sister, Amy, and me, especially. We really missed her presence. We have kept in touch by writing letters, and we occasionally talk over the telephone.

Two years later, in June 1992, Kathy came back to visit our family for a month. Even though we were two years older and had changed in some ways, we still felt that immediate closeness that we had known before.

Today, she is 20 years old and is in medical school in Berlin. She is doing exceptionally well and expects to graduate in a few years with her medical degree.

Kathy added so much joy to my life. She was the older sister I never had, and she was a friend that can never be replaced. I still keep in touch with Kathy, and I always will.

Chance brought us together, but love made us lifelong friends.

Source: Reprinted courtesy of Tuscaloosa News, Tuscaloosa, Alabama, April 12, 1994, p. 8A.

Task 1.18 Postreading

TWO-WAY LEARNING

Step 1. List in your notebook all the things that Elizabeth and her family learned from Kathy.
Step 2. Now write down all the things that Kathy learned from Elizabeth and her family.
Step 3. Write down why Elizabeth considers Kathy her "sister."
Step 4. Explain in writing why the fall of the Berlin Wall was so important to everyone in the story.
Step 5. In your notebook, answer these questions: Have you ever had a lifelong friend from another culture? If so, who was that person, and what were the circumstances that brought you together?
Step 6. Compare your answers with other people. Add to your answers if you wish.

Task 1.19 Prelistening

EXPANDING YOUR BACKGROUND KNOWLEDGE

Before you listen to the tape, find out about the recent history of Afghanistan. Learn about the coup that changed society there. Take notes on index cards or notebook paper. Discuss your notes with three or four others.

Task 1.20 Listening

SEEKING FAMILY DETAILS

As you listen, seek details about the man's life. Write down as many details as you can locate. Make your list as long as possible. (Hints: Look for information about his job, family, home, education, etc.)

Your tape has **"From Government Official to Immigrant,"** by an Afghan immigrant (interviewed by Janet Robinson). Used with permission.

Task 1.21 Postlistening

COUNTING THE BLESSINGS

Step 1. Take notes on the following:
- **a.** What kind of work did the man do before the coup in Afghanistan?
- **b.** Who took his place in that job, and why?
- **c.** Why do you think he sent his sons away to Pakistan?

d. What kinds of work did the family find in Pakistan?
e. What did the man do to ensure the survival of his family (at least five actions)?

Step 2. Discuss with others why the man does not feel he has experienced discrimination. Give all the evidence you can.

Step 3. In the United States and some other countries, there is a saying: "Some people see the glass as half full, and others see it as half empty." Discuss with others: What does this saying mean to you in light of the story of the man from Afghanistan? Do you think he sees the glass as half full, or do you think he sees the glass as half empty?

Task 1.22 Prereading

FEELING FEAR AND HESITATION

List all the times you have felt fear and hesitation. Compare your list with the list of one other person. Were the situations similar? Did any of the situations relate to moving to or visiting a new country?

Task 1.23 Reading

CONFRONTING THE FEAR AND HESITATION

As you read, make a special note of how Teeda and Vitou confront the fear and hesitation they feel. Take notes about all their "weapons"—the things they use and do to combat negative feelings.

That's what I want to be

by JoAn D. Criddle

TEEDA:

We were scared—no, terrified. It was March 1980, the start of a new life for us. Entering this land of opportunity as young adults with less than ninth grade educations, my husband and I felt deep concern, especially about earning a living.

In 1979, Vitou and I fled Cambodia, then waited in Thai refugee camps for more than five months before sponsorship was arranged and our papers cleared for emigration. Finally, the impossible was realized; we landed in America.

Disembarking from the Pan Am flight from Bangkok, we nervously entered the terminal at San Francisco International Airport with my bewildered mother **in tow.** Despite jet lag, the three of us wandered around the building, absorbing sights, smells, and sounds of America while we waited for our continuing flight to Sacramento. Vitou spied mechanics working on a United Airlines plane. He watched for some time, then turned to me and said, "That's what I want to be."

. . . The Khmer Rouge robbed us of the years in which Vitou and I should have gained the basic skills needed to function successfully as adults in the modern world. Instead, we spent our teen years in backbreaking labor and in trying to survive one more day by outwitting our captors. Thinking about a future had seemed pointless when each day might be our last.

Then in January 1979, when Vietnam broke the Khmer Rouge stranglehold over Cambodia, all our attention shifted to escape attempts and the struggle to find food. Fourteen months after we began our escape, we were finally entering America. For five terror-filled years the future had seemed a void. We now faced that future and felt ill equipped.

Vitou was twenty-one years old when we arrived in California. I was nineteen. We had limited schooling, and our English was almost nonexistent. We had escaped with little more than the **tattered** clothes on our backs, almost no financial resources, few physical or emotional reserves, and limited knowledge of how to succeed in America. Our one real asset was determination. At times even that faltered.

Neither of us had ever held a paying job. Our years of hard labor in the jungles and rice paddies had not equipped us with job skills needed in this technologically advanced nation. We felt overwhelmed. Where to start? How to proceed? I wasn't sure we had the energy to even try. Yet here was Vitou fantasizing about a career; we'd be lucky to get **stoop** labor.

. . . We hated to settle for a lifetime of labor at minimum wage, but we were afraid to voice what we really desired, even to ourselves, let alone to our sponsors. The idea of expecting anything but **menial** work seemed wishful at best and childish in the face of **stark** reality.

[Our sponsors explained about the three years of government financial help for resettlement and education.] Three years is not long to learn another language, adjust to a new culture, acquire marketable job skills, find employment, and become self-supporting. Nonetheless, we felt embarrassed to accept handouts for even that long from a nation that had already granted us freedom and safety. Besides, we had our pride; formerly we'd been a self-sufficient, middle-class Cambodian family.

. . . Finally one of the sponsors said, "Forget about money, language limitations and all that. Tell us what you would like to be if those weren't issues. Tell us what you planned to be had war never come to Cambodia. Then let's see how much of that dream is feasible."

Timidly I admitted that before the war, I had always planned to go to college and perhaps even try for a master's or a doctorate. Few Cambodians had attained these levels of education and certainly not many women, but my father had encouraged my aspirations when he was alive.

With hesitation, Vitou then shared his dream with our sponsors. Fascinated by machines since childhood, he'd always wanted to be a mechanic or perhaps earn an engineering degree. He wanted to repair or perhaps design cars and airplanes.

There. It was out. We waited for our unrealistic hopes to be dashed. Instead, a long, serious discussion began about options, only part of which we understood. . . .

. . . From then on, I could truly say, as I often have since, "In America I never felt poor even when we had nothing. Here we had freedom and opportunity. We could become whatever we were willing to work for." . . . Those who have never been enslaved can never fully appreciate what rare gifts freedom and opportunity are. Being poor is merely an inconvenience when you know it need be only temporary.

Teeda and Vitou in the center, with others, after the citizenship ceremony.

Source: JoAn D. Criddle, Bamboo & Butterflies: From Refugee to Citizen. Dixon, Calif.: East/West BRIDGE Publishing House, 1992, pp. 79–83. Used with permission.

Task 1.24 Postreading

SEPARATING THE PLUSSES AND THE MINUSES

Step 1. In the chart below, list the plusses (the positive things Teeda and Vitou brought to America and the positive things their sponsors and the U.S. government provided). Also list the minuses (the negatives, or Teeda's and Vitou's self-perceived lacks).

A BALANCE SHEET FOR TEEDA AND VITOU

PLUS FACTORS	MINUS FACTORS
a. ____________	a. ____________
b. ____________	b. ____________
c. ____________	c. ____________
d. ____________	d. ____________
e. ____________	e. ____________
f. ____________	f. ____________
g. ____________	g. ____________

Step 2. Discuss with others as you compare your charts: Which side of the chart has more information? That is, are there more plusses than minuses? Or are there more minuses than plusses?

Step 3. Discuss: What helped Teeda to see that she would never be really poor in America? What changed her attitude? Have you ever been in an "enslaved" country? If so, what did you feel like, and how long were you there?

CULTURAL PATTERN 4: UNDERSTANDING CULTURES MORE CLEARLY, STEP BY STEP

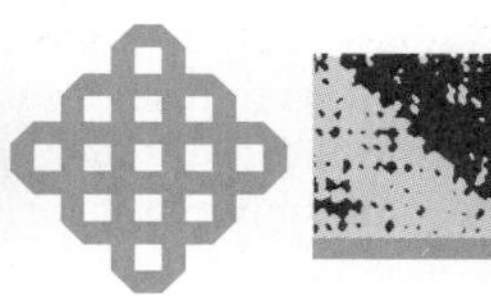

LEARNING STRATEGY

Forming Concepts: Scanning (reading quickly to find specific ideas) helps you identify important things and focuses your reading.

Task 1.25 Prereading

SCANNING

Use the learning strategy of SCANNING for the five steps in cultural understanding *before* you read the rest of the whole article. Highlight each step by circling it.

IT WORKS! Learning Strategy: Guessing from the Context

Task 1.26 Reading

GUESSING AS NEEDED

Now read the article slowly and carefully. While reading the passage, do not look up all the words you do not know. Be sure to *guess from the context.*

Steps in cultural understanding

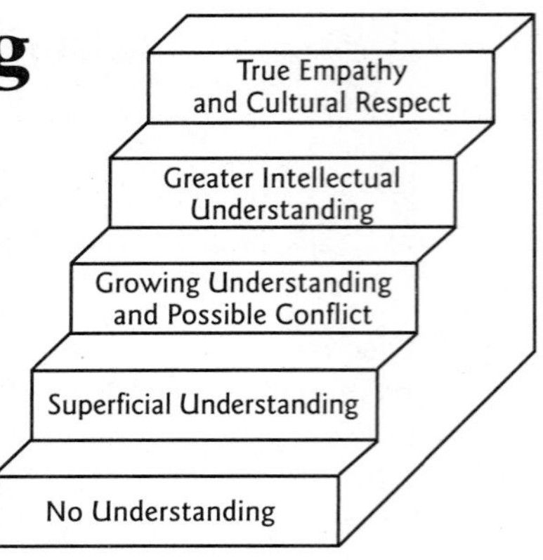

Steps in Cultural Understanding

Like learning a language, developing cultural understanding occurs step by step over time. It does not happen all at once, like switching on a light. Development of cultural consciousness is a process that starts at the stage of no understanding and moves, in the best case, to the stage of true empathy and cultural respect.

You might attain a particular stage of cultural attunement and then slip back to an earlier level when you are under great stress. You might even jump ahead temporarily to a more advanced stage, but it is not really "yours" until you have consolidated it and until you have felt comfortable in it for several weeks or months.

Five stages of cultural understanding are shown here:

Stage One: No Understanding. This level involves no awareness of the new culture. The culture might as well be on an unknown planet in outer space. The person does not know anyone from the culture and has encountered few if any basic facts about the culture.

Stage Two: Superficial Understanding. This level consists of awareness of very superficial (shallow, on-the-surface, visible) aspects of the culture—frequently negative aspects. At this stage of cultural awareness, the person knows a few basic facts. These facts stand out and often serve as the basis of *stereotypes.* Stereotypes are defined as common myths, frequently containing a grain of truth but typically exaggerated, about a given culture and its people. Stereotypes are frequently transmitted through the media: TV, movies, newspapers, magazines.

The picture above shows a stereotype about North Americans. It depicts North Americans as fat, white, foolish-looking tourists, wearing flowered shirts with shorts for the man and tight pants for the woman, carrying cameras, and letting dollar bills gush from their pockets indiscriminately. This stereotype may reflect some tourists from North America, but certainly not all of them. North Americans are not the only ones who suffer from stereotypes. A stereotype of Northern Europeans is that they are cold and unfeeling. Latin Americans are stereotyped as being friendly but lazy. Australian men are viewed as hard drinkers who enjoy nothing better than shrimp on the barbie (or **barbecue**).

Stereotypes are offensive because they imply that all people from a certain culture have the same characteristics. At this stage of cultural awareness, when stereotypes are keenly felt, the person is highly *ethnocentric* (focusing on his or her own culture as the norm of what is "right" and comparing the new culture with the "better" culture back home). Some touches of culture shock might be evident here, especially rejecting the culture on account of the stereotypes.

Stage Three: Growing Understanding and Possible Conflict. This is the stage where the learner begins to be aware of more subtle, sometimes less visible, traits in the culture. For example, a student learns that a given culture focuses on the family far more than on getting things accomplished. He or she begins to appreciate the huge importance of family values in this culture. Once sensitized, the student becomes increasingly aware that family values and family ties **infuse** the whole political, economic, and religious system of the country.

This understanding helps the person to see why things operate the way they do, but such an awareness does not always bring acceptance. The situation might still seem very frustrating, irrational, and disconcerting to the person who is becoming aware of a specific culture. In Stage Three, there is greater understanding than in Stage Two, but the person is still ethnocentric, comparing the culture that is "new" to his or her "old" home culture—and usually feeling that the "old" culture is much better. The individual experiences many cultural conflicts and may actually go through severe culture shock at this stage.

Stage Four: Greater Intellectual Understanding. At this stage, the learner begins to comprehend

Cultural Stereotypes

intellectually the people in the culture, yet there is still little emotional empathy; the person cannot "feel what it is like" to be a member of the culture. The learner thus starts to see things intellectually through the eyes of the "culture bearers" at least part of the time but cannot really feel the same way they feel. The learner begins to shed ethnocentrism a little bit and starts to understand more deeply. The person knows why things are done the way they are done and accepts these things with less irritation.

The learner objectively comprehends the beliefs and actions of the people in the culture. The comfort level is higher, and the person does not complain extensively about cultural differences. (Naturally, however, many people who have grown up in the new culture actually complain—good-naturedly or otherwise—about their own culture, just as we might complain about our own. This normal, home-grown cultural self-criticism is different from criticizing the new culture when one is not part of it.) Culture shock is **receding** at this stage, because the individual is trying hard to understand the culture, at least from an intellectual viewpoint.

Stage Five: True Empathy and Cultural Respect. This level is the height of cultural awareness. To attain this level, the learner must actually live in the culture for some time. The amount of time the learner must live in the culture to reach Stage Five is variable, depending on the individual. At the fifth stage, the learner does not just see things intellectually from the viewpoint of the culture some or most of the time. Instead he or she actually *feels* part of the culture, respects the culture fully, and empathizes emotionally with those who have lived all their lives in the culture. Any previous culture shock has been replaced by a feeling of much greater comfort.

In summary, here are the stages in the growth of cultural consciousness:

Steps in Cultural Understanding

1. No understanding—does not know anyone from the culture, knows few if any facts.
2. Superficial understanding—knows some superficial facts and stereotypes.
3. Growing understanding and possible conflict—is aware of more subtle traits but may experience cultural conflict; probably believes own culture is superior.
4. Greater intellectual understanding—understands the culture intellectually but not emotionally.
5. True empathy and respect—understands the culture both intellectually and emotionally; can feel what the people in the culture feel.

Source: Contains some concepts selected from Robert G. Hanvey, "Cross-Cultural Awareness," in Louise F. Luce, ed., The Spanish-Speaking World: An Anthology of Cross-Cultural Perspectives, Lincolnwood, Ill.: National Textbook Co., 1992, p. 22 ff.; and Jan Gaston, Cross-Cultural Awareness Teaching Techniques, Brattleboro, Vt.: ProLingua Associates, 1984.

Task 1.27 Postreading

CHECKING YOUR UNDERSTANDING

Fill in the blanks below with the appropriate answers.

Step 1. Stage One shows ________________ understanding at all for the new culture.

Step 2. In Stage Two, the level of understanding can be described as ________________. At this stage, cultural understanding is filled with ________________, which are common beliefs about people and cultures that are often exaggerated and strange, even though they may contain a little bit of truth. An example of this is: ________________.

Step 3. At the third stage, the person begins to comprehend ________________ traits within the culture. Nevertheless, there may still be many things that seem ________________ or ________________. The person still thinks the ________________ culture is much better than the ________________ culture.

Step 4. When the person reaches Stage Four, there is a greater ________________ awareness of the reasons why the culture works the way it does, but no deep emotional understanding or ________________ for the culture. The person still does not feel that he or she is of the culture.

Step 5. At Stage Five, something special happens: the person now feels ________________ of the culture and has developed both ________________ and ________________ for the people of the culture. To reach this stage, the person must ________________.

Task 1.28 Expanding Your Knowledge

PRACTICING THE NUMBERS

Answer these questions by filling in the blanks with the right numbers of the stages of cultural awareness:

_____ **a.** Which stage brings only intellectual understanding but no emotional empathy?

_____ **b.** Which stage shows no understanding at all of the culture?

_____ **c.** At which stage does the person start to feel the same way as people in the new culture?

_____ **d.** What stage features stereotypes and superficial understanding of the culture?

_____ **e.** Which stage has moved away from stereotypes but still has a lot of cultural conflict?

Task 1.29 Expanding Your Knowledge

ASSESSING YOUR CULTURAL UNDERSTANDING

You are learning English and cultures that use English; you might even be in an English-speaking culture right now. What is your general level of cultural understanding of the English-speaking culture(s)?

IT WORKS! Learning Strategy: Assessing Your Ability

CULTURAL PATTERN 5: EXAMPLES OF STEREOTYPES AND ASSUMPTIONS

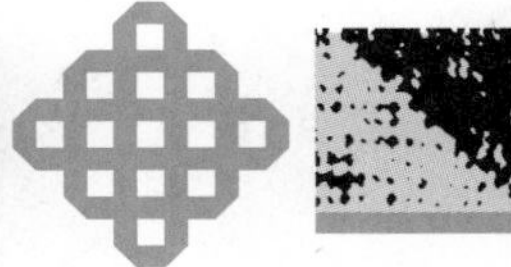

CULTURE CLIP!
Stereotypes of U.S. Mainstream Culture

Here are some typical stereotypes of U.S. mainstream culture often held by people from other countries:

- rich
- friendly
- superficial relationships
- don't care about family
- don't care about old people
- loud, rude, like to shout
- talk a lot but don't say much
- think they are the experts
- aggressive
- believe in personal control, not fate
- in a hurry
- dislike authority
- driven by money, possessions
- competitive
- adventurous
- patriotic
- future-oriented
- believe in decisions and action
- spend too much on themselves
- generous to others
- hardworking but undisciplined
- like to improve themselves
- direct and open
- immature
- ignorant about the rest of the world
- racially prejudiced but believe in equality
- promiscuous
- risk-taking
- religious but not always church-going

Add others here:

- ______________________
- ______________________
- ______________________
- ______________________

Do you agree the stereotypes above describe U.S. culture accurately?

What are *your own cultural values* for each point above? Discuss with others.

Threads

The best antidote to stereotyping may be found in the difficulties each ethnic group encounters in agreeing on their own ethnic behavior.

ESL Teacher Jan Clarke

Task 1.30 Prereading

UNDERSTANDING HUMAN NATURE

Discuss with others: When you fear *you* are not good enough, do you ever ridicule, laugh about, or say bad things about *someone else* to make yourself feel better? When does this happen? Give some examples, and get ready to read about one!

LEARNING STRATEGY

Understanding and Using Emotions: Delve into the motivations behind actions if you want to understand people and cultures.

Task 1.31 Reading

THINKING ABOUT REASONS

As you read, consider reasons why Helen, Theresa, and Ralph might make fun of other people.

Typical Americans

by Gish Jen

Now, America. For the first few months, she could hardly sit without thinking how she might be wearing out her irreplaceable clothes. How careful she had to be! Theresa would **traipse** all over, searching out that elusive brother of hers; Helen walked as little and as lightly as she could, sparing her shoes, that they might last until the Nationalists saved her country and she could go home again. She studied the way she walked too, lightly—why should she struggle with English? She wrote her parents during class, every day hoping for an answer that never came. She went to Chinatown three times a week, thinking of it as one more foreign quarter of Shanghai . . . . She learned to cook, so that she'd have Chinese food to eat. When she could not have Chinese food, she did not eat. . . .

This could not go on forever. Eventually, faith faltering, Helen studied harder, walked more, bought new clothes, wrote her parents less. She did continue to spend whole afternoons simply sitting still, staring, as though hoping to be visited by ghosts, or by a truly wasting disease; but she also developed a liking for American magazines, American newspapers, American radio. . . . And she married Ralph [a Chinese immigrant], officially accepting what seemed already true—that she had indeed crossed a violent, black ocean; and that it was time to make herself as at home in her exile as she could. . . .

Typical Pete

Entertainment: Ralph took to imitating Pete's [the superintendent of the apartment building] walk. He'd slump, a finger cleaning his ear, only to have Theresa gamely cry out, "No, *no like this,*" and add a shuffle, turning out her knees as Helen laughed. They studied the way Pete blew his nose, that they might get it right; they studied his sneeze, his laugh, the self-important way he flipped through his calendar. "Well, now, let me have some look-see," growled Theresa. "Typical Pete!" Ralph roared in approval. "Typical, typical Pete...."

. . . And pretty soon, no one knew quite how, "typical Pete" turned "typical American" turned typical American this, typical American that. "Typical American no-good," Ralph would say; Theresa, "typical American just-don't-know-how-to-get-along;" and Helen, wistfully, "typical American just-want-to-be-the-center-of-things." They were sure, of course, that they wouldn't "become wild" here in America, where there was "no one to control them." Yet they were more sure still as they shook their heads over a clerk who shortchanged them ("typical American no-morals!"). Over a neighbor who snapped his key in his door lock ("typical American use-brute-force!"). Or what about that other neighbor's kid, who claimed the opposite of a Democrat to be a **pelican**? ("Peckin?" said Ralph. "A kind of bird," explained Theresa; then he laughed too. "Typical American just-dumb!")

Source: From Typical American.

Task 1.32 Postreading

LOOKING AT THE REASONS

Write your answers in your notebook and then discuss with a partner.

Step 1. Why did Helen, Theresa, and Ralph make fun of the superintendent of the building?

Step 2. How did their ridicule of one man become stereotypes of many people?

Step 3. Were these stereotypes fair and accurate descriptions of most Americans? Explain your answer.

Step 4. How positive do you think Helen felt about *herself* at the times when she was most involved in ridiculing Americans?

Step 5. Do you think Helen and her companions would maintain the stereotypes they developed of Americans after living in the United States for four or more years? Why or why not?

Step 6. Is there such a thing as a "typical American" or a "typical Frenchman" or a "typical Japanese" or a "typical Canadian" or a "typical Arabic (or English) speaker"? Explain your answer.

Task 1.33 Prelistening

PREDICTING WHAT PEOPLE MIGHT THINK

Discuss with others: What stereotypes might a German person have of North Americans? What stereotypes might North Americans have of Germans?

Task 1.34 Listening

IT WORKS!
Learning Strategy:
Empathizing with
Someone Else

EMPATHIZING WITH THE PERSON

As you listen, catch the feelings of Hans. Try to feel what he is feeling.

Your tape has **"Stereotypes Everywhere,"** by Hans Kaufman (interviewed by Catherine L. Callender). Used with permission.

Stereotype of Germans

Task 1.35 Postlistening

DECODING THE MESSAGE

Step 1. What are the stereotypes that Americans had of Germans in this story?
Step 2. What is the single, general stereotype that Hans had of America?
Step 3. How can a person alter his or her stereotypes of a culture?
Step 4. Discuss your answers with someone else.

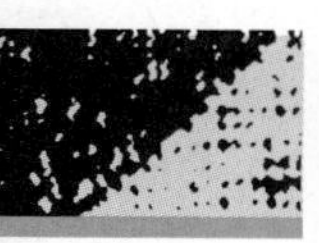

CULTURAL PATTERN 6: WHEN THE VIEW IS SHOCKING

Task 1.36 Prereading

Threads

Genius is the capacity to see ten things where the ordinary person sees one.

Poet Ezra Pound

BRAINSTORMING AND VOTING

Step 1. Brainstorm all the possible meanings and ideas your group can generate about culture shock. Write them on a large sheet of paper.
Step 2. In the group, raise your hands to indicate how many of you think you might have experienced culture shock.

Task 1.37 Reading

IDENTIFYING THE FEATURES

As you listen, write down all the features or characteristics of culture shock that you hear.

Two views of culture shock

Culture shock is anxiety resulting from the loss of commonly understood signs and symbols of social interaction, says Peter Adler, a well-known writer and expert on culture shock. In simpler words, *people feel culture shock when all the expected, familiar hints and helps are stripped away.* Suddenly they do not know what to do, how to act, or what in the world to think. There are two major views of culture shock: the disease view and the self-awareness view.

The Disease View of Culture Shock. One perspective on culture shock is the *disease view.* The culture-shocked person experiences a breakdown in communication, is unable to cope, and feels isolated and lost. The culture-shocked person thus develops a number of defensive (and sometimes offensive) attitudes and behaviors to protect the mind from the confusion of an entirely new situation. In this view, the culture-shocked person is a helpless victim. The only things this victim can do to "get well" are to adjust to the new culture somehow, or else to leave the culture quickly.

In this disease view, people can experience many different emotional and mental difficulties. They can become extremely frustrated, angry, and rejecting of the new culture. They consider the host country bad, ridiculous, stupid, or hopeless—precisely because they themselves feel bad, ridiculous, stupid, or hopeless. Culture-shocked people may start to glorify the home country; suddenly everything about the native land is wonderful compared to this terrible new place! Some culture-shocked people fear physical contact with anyone or anything from the new culture, no matter how safe or clean. Feelings of helplessness about delays and confusions can turn rapidly into resentment. People in culture shock may feel **contaminated,** tricked, deceived, injured, or ignored—or all of these.

Culture shock not only has psychological and social aspects, but it also has repercussions in terms of physical health. People can become physically ill from the stress of culture shock. Ulcers, headaches, stomach aches, back aches, the flu—these and hundreds of other physical symptoms can often be traced back to an underlying culture shock condition.

One important aspect of the disease concept of culture shock is "reduced personality." The person cannot speak the language well, and therefore communications are limited. Some of the areas of the most limited communication are usually personal feelings and psychological needs. If adults cannot express these things, they feel like small children or awkward teenagers. Experiencing a "reduced personality" can bring shame and anger.

The Self-Awareness View of Culture Shock. The disease view of culture shock, in which the person is an unwilling victim, is not the only view of culture shock. There is another, much more positive concept of culture shock, says Adler. This second concept is called the *self-awareness view of culture shock.* Culture shock can be part of a positive learning experience. Culture shock, if handled well, can lead to profound self-awareness and growth.

Adler says that positive cross-cultural learning experiences typically:

- involve change and movement from one cultural frame of reference to another;
- are personally and uniquely important to the individual;
- force the person into some form of self-examination;
- involve severe frustration, anxiety, and personal pain, at least for a while;
- cause the person to deal with relationships and processes related to his or her role as an outsider;
- encourage the person to try new attitudes and behaviors; and
- allow the person to compare and contrast constantly.

Out of such an experience, the individual—let's call him Li-Yin—may learn that being warm and open may elicit the same behavior from others in the new culture. This experience may help bring back lost pieces of himself. Li-Yin may learn that trying to communicate, even though making mistakes in public, can help him get to know people. He may find out that being tolerant about people's awkward responses toward him will ease everyone's anxiety. This in turn might enable people in the new culture to want to accept Li-Yin. He might begin to recognize that the old culture's ways are not perfect and that the new culture has something he can learn. Li-Yin might find in the new culture that he can tolerate the cultural behaviors that at first seemed crazy and annoying.

The strong, creative person can deal with culture shock positively, instead of sinking into steady complaints about the culture, wallowing in very real physical ailments, or running away at the first opportunity. Culture shock can become an opportunity for growth.

LEARNING STRATEGY

Personalizing: Reread a passage to see how it links with your own personal experience.

Task 1.38 Postreading

RELATING CULTURE SHOCK TO YOUR OWN EXPERIENCE

Step 1. Look back at your notes from the reading (or if you have to, look back at the reading itself). Now, on a separate sheet, group the signs of culture shock according to categories like the following. They are the main labels; put examples or details under each one. Add other labels if you want.

POSSIBLE SIGNS OF CULTURE SHOCK

GROUP 1	GROUP 2	GROUP 3	GROUP 4
Physical problems	Offensive behavior	Negative attitudes about self	Negative attitudes about the culture

Threads

Civilization is a movement and not a condition, a voyage and not a harbor.

Historian Arnold Toynbee

Step 2. Circle any of the signs of culture shock (in Step 1) that you have personally experienced. Note where and when you had these experiences.

Step 3. Did you ever go through the positive cross-cultural growth experience Adler describes, in which culture shock is a main part? If so, describe it.

Step 4. Now discuss your answers with someone else who has traveled and lived abroad. See if that person's experience of culture shock relates in any way to yours. To do this, you must listen actively and carefully. Write down any similarities and differences.

Task 1.39 Prelistening

DOING YOUR GEOGRAPHY

Step 1. Look up Korea, California, and Alabama on a map of the world.
Step 2. Calculate the number of miles between each point and write it in the appropriate spaces below (and in Step 3).

Korea to California: __________ miles

Korea to Alabama: __________ miles

California to Alabama: __________ miles

Step 3. Discuss with others how a Korean student who had grown up in Korea *might* feel in California (________ miles from Korea) and in Alabama (________ miles from Korea).

LEARNING STRATEGY

Understanding and Using Emotions: In reading, search for feelings that the person expresses, not just facts.

Task 1.40 Listening

FINDING FEELINGS AND FACTS

Look for the feelings as well as the facts as you listen to this story.

Your tape has **"My Experiences with Culture Shock,"** by Young Ye Park-Oh. Used with permission.

Young (second from left) with international friends.

Task 1.41 Postlistening

EXAMINING THE SITUATION

Step 1. Write down three things that made Young's initial stay in California so difficult from a cultural point of view.
Step 2. Write down three things that caused Young's move to Alabama more positive from a cultural point of view.
Step 3. What did Young herself contribute to making this a positive cross-cultural learning experience?
Step 4. Why do you think Young is still suffering somewhat?
Step 5. Is there anything you might suggest to Young?
Step 6. Have you ever experienced any of Young's feelings? Explain.
Step 7. Discuss your thoughts with someone else or with a small group. What can you learn from each other?

WORD PATTERNS

Task 1.42 Wordbuilding

BREAKING DOWN WORDS AND STARRING FAMILIAR WORDS

You probably met many new words in this chapter, either in the book or on the tape. Some of the words have been marked for you throughout this chapter (see list below).

a. Circle any of the words below you can understand simply by breaking the word down into parts.
b. Put a star (*) next to any that look or sound like a word you already know.

barbecue—the grill on which meat is cooked, usually outdoors
compassion—the act of being sympathetic to other's distress and the desire to alleviate it
comprehensive—complete
contaminated—poisoned
entertaining—providing entertainment or fun
generating—originating or producing
iceberg—a large floating mass of ice detached from a glacier
infuse—to soak in liquid, to pour in, to inspire
in tow—attached by a rope and pulled along (figurative)

intricately—in a complicated way
menial—related to servants
mosque—a building used for public worship by Muslims
nonprescription—able to be bought without a medical doctor's order
pelican—a sea bird [speaker means "Republican" in this case]
prejudice—a belief formed in the absence of sufficient information; a judgment or opinion formed in advance
receding—drawing back
refinement—improvement, development
relishing—enjoying
repugnant—hostile or antagonistic
sophisticated—more developed, refined, or subtle
sophistication—the state of being more developed, refined, or subtle
stark—barren, plain
stoop—involving the act of bending one's back
tattered—ragged
traipse—to walk over a long distance without following a fixed route
violated—broken, intruded upon, harmed
Westernized—having qualities native to the West

Task 1.43 Wordbuilding

PUTTING WORDS IN THE BANK

In the following box, list other words from this chapter that are new to you and explain what they mean:

NEW WORDS	YOUR DEFINITIONS
______________________	______________________
______________________	______________________
______________________	______________________
______________________	______________________
______________________	______________________
______________________	______________________
______________________	______________________

CHECKING YOUR SUCCESS

Task 1.44 Evaluating

REVIEWING THE OBJECTIVES AND RATING YOURSELF

IT WORKS! Learning Strategy: Assessing Your Ability

Circle YES or NO.

Can you . . .

• describe the differences between everyday and "sophisticated" culture?	YES	NO
• identify the parts of the cultural iceberg?	YES	NO
• describe the steps in cultural understanding?	YES	NO
• describe two different views of culture shock?	YES	NO
• analyze several people's experiences of life in a new culture?	YES	NO
• use many new learning strategies to make your studying easier?	YES	NO

Task 1.45 Evaluating

CHECKING ATTITUDES

Now that you have participated in the cultural learning tasks in this chapter, how do you feel about them? Use the following list. Circle the adjectives that indicate your feelings.

interested	*uninterested*
excited	*bored*
unafraid	*fearful*
eager	*inhibited*
open	*closed*
comfortable	*uncomfortable*
happy	*unhappy*
relaxed	*anxious*

If you circled more than five adjectives on the right-hand side, you *might* have a barrier to overcome regarding certain cultural activities—or perhaps language problems are getting in the way. What can you do to participate in these activities fully? Discuss your answers with someone else, and get help if you need it.

If you circled more than five adjectives on the left-hand side, welcome to the exciting world of culture! Your energy is high, and you will be open to many new ideas. Discuss your answers with someone else, and try to pass along that spark of excitement.

WHERE TO GO FOR MORE INFORMATION

Adler, Peter S. (1972). Culture shock and the cross-cultural learning experience. *Readings in Intercultural Communication,* 2, 6–21.

Althern, Gary. (1988). *American ways: a guide for foreigners in the United States.* Yarmouth, Me.: Intercultural Press.

Andromidas, Charles, Arntraud Harman, & Michael Mercil. (1980). *Living in the U.S.A.* Washington, D.C.: Youth for Understanding.

Banks, James A. (1994). *Multiethnic education: Theory and practice.* 3rd ed. Boston: Allyn & Bacon.

Banks, James A., & Cherry A. McGee Banks (1993). *Multicultural education: Issues and perspectives.* 2nd ed. Boston: Allyn & Bacon.

Batchelder, Donald, & Elizabeth G. Warner (1977). *Beyond experience: The experiential approach to cross-cultural education.* Brattleboro, Vt.: Experiment in International Living.

Bullivant, Brian M. (1984). *Pluralism: Cultural maintenance and evolution.* Clevedon, Avon, England: Multilingual Matters.

Criddle, JoAn D. (1992). *Bamboo and butterflies: From refugee to citizen.* Dixon, Calif.: East/West BRIDGE Publishing House.

Gaston, Jan. (1984). *Cultural awareness teaching techniques.* Brattleboro, Vt.: ProLingua Associates.

Geertz, Clifford. (1973). *The interpretation of cultures.* New York: Basic Books.

Hall, Edward T. (1969). *The hidden dimension.* Garden City, New York: Doubleday/ Anchor.

Hall, Edward T. (1973). *The silent language.* Garden City, New York: Doubleday/Anchor.

Hall, Edward T., & Mildred Reed Hall, (1990). *Understanding cultural differences.* Yarmouth, Me.: Intercultural Press.

Kearney, Edward N., Mary Ann Kearney, & JoAnn Crandall (1984). *The American way: An introduction to American culture.* Englewood Cliffs, N.J.: Prentice-Hall.

Putsch, Margaret D., ed. (1986). *Multicultural education: A crosscultural training approach.* Yarmouth, Me.: Intercultural Press.

Seelye, H. Ned. (1984). *Teaching culture.* Skokie, Ill.: National Textbook Co.

Stewart, Edward C., & Milton J. Bennett (1991). *American cultural patterns.* Rev. ed. Yarmouth, Me.: Intercultural Press.

Weeks, William H., Paul B. Pedersen, & Richard W. Brislin, eds. (1990). *A manual of structured experiences for cross-cultural learning.* Yarmouth, Me.: Intercultural Press.

Time and Space

2

CHAPTER

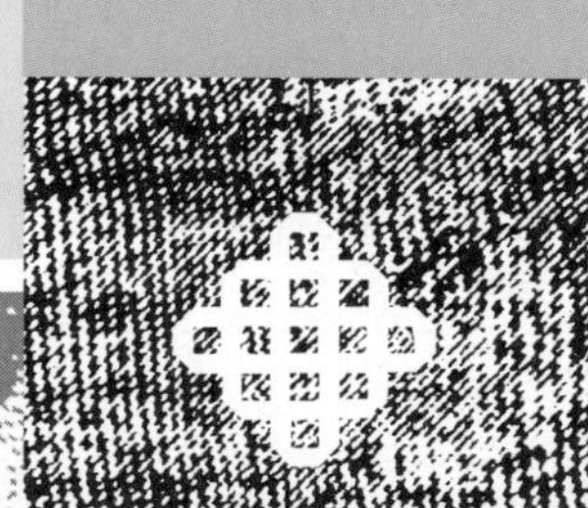

INTRODUCTION

PREVIEW QUESTIONS

1. What are two main ways cultures look at time?
2. Why do cultures look at time differently?
3. How do different concepts of time affect relationships and work?
4. What is personal space?
5. What cultural differences exist in terms of space?

Time and space are coiled
like some unimaginable ***DNA,****
pregnant with both
possibility and certainty.

—*Science fiction writer Sheri S. Tepper*

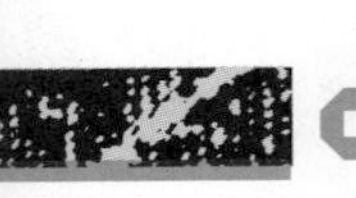

PATTERNS IN THIS CHAPTER

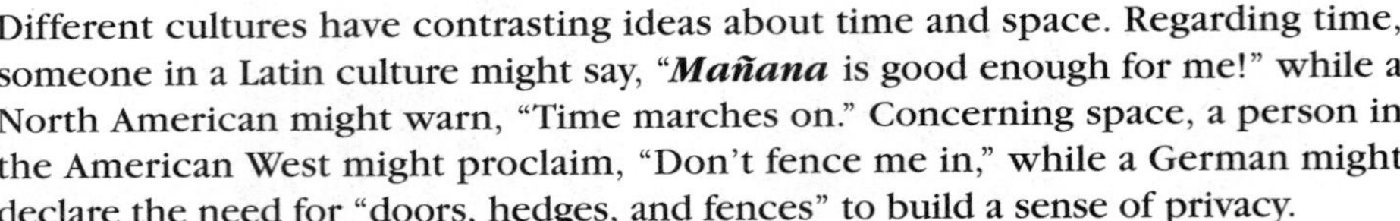

Threads

The present: catch it if you can.

Novelist Annie Dillard

Different cultures have contrasting ideas about time and space. Regarding time, someone in a Latin culture might say, "***Mañana*** is good enough for me!" while a North American might warn, "Time marches on." Concerning space, a person in the American West might proclaim, "Don't fence me in," while a German might declare the need for "doors, hedges, and fences" to build a sense of privacy.

This chapter describes time and space in cultures around the world. The main patterns deal with two key ways of looking at time, reasons for cultures to choose these views, ways that different concepts of time influence relationships and work, the meaning of personal space, and cultural differences regarding personal space. Throughout this chapter you will find stories of real people caught in the cultural net of time and space.

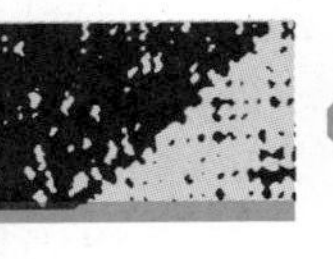

YOUR SUCCESS PATTERNS IN THIS CHAPTER

Using your growing English skills during this chapter, you will be able to:

- describe two cultural modes of looking at time;
- explain why cultures look at time differently;
- discuss how different concepts of time influence relationships and work;
- explain the concept of personal space;
- describe cultural differences in space; and
- use many new learning strategies to make your studying easier.

---

*Words in text set in bold type are listed alphabetically and defined in the Word Patterns section on page 63 of this chapter.

Task 2.1 Evaluating

YOUR SUCCESS PATTERNS IN THIS CHAPTER

IT WORKS! Learning Strategy: Assessing Your Ability

THINKING ABOUT YOURSELF

Speed

Step 1. Assess your current ability by circling the actions above that you can do *now.*

Step 2. Which actions did you *not* circle? These are the actions to which you can pay most attention in this chapter. (If you did not circle any, this chapter offers you enormous benefits in learning about cultural concepts of time and space.)

Task 2.2 Expanding Your Knowledge

IT WORKS! Learning Strategy: Noticing Your Feelings

TAKING YOUR TIME

Respond to the following questions by circling T for TRUE and F for FALSE (for you personally).

1.	Time is a source of pressure, a **taskmaster** that demands accomplishment.	T	F
2.	Time is a limited commodity and must be used wisely.	T	F
3.	I should avoid wasting my time talking with friends or "goofing off."	T	F
4.	Time seems to be more of an enemy than a friend to me.	T	F
5.	If I make an appointment, I must keep it.	T	F
6.	Time is a flexible thing that stretches if I want to enjoy the company of family or friends.	T	F
7.	Time is adjustable, allowing me to shift appointments freely.	T	F
8.	I can drop my work for a while to talk on the phone or drink coffee or tea with a friend.	T	F
9.	The things written on my calendar don't necessarily have to occur.	T	F
10.	Time is my servant, not my master.	T	F

Threads

The past is not a package that one can lay away.

Poet Emily Dickinson

Give yourself one point for any "true" responses for #1–5 and one point for any "false" responses for #6–10.

Write your score here: __________

If you have a score of 5 or more, you are probably from a culture that values using time for achievements and accomplishments. If you have a score of less than 5, you are probably from a culture that values having time to enhance your relationships.

CULTURE CLIP!

Some cultures are literally established on the concept of time. Here's an example. The Mayan tribe of Central America—an ancient tribe that still remains today in areas of Guatemala—focused its religion on the concept of time, *kin(h)*. Although their neighbors the Aztecs were time-obsessed, the Maya were even more concerned about time. The Maya developed ideas of religious time and solar time, which were quite different. Like the Aztecs, the Maya used the religious time unit of 260 days, divided into 13 periods × 20 days. These units were combinations of the gods of the 13 numbers and the gods of the 20 day-signs. These were further combined into a period of 7,200 days, which served as a religious period to explain events. Yet the Maya, like the Aztecs, also had a solar year of 365 days divided into 18 periods of 20 days, plus five extra days. Solar years were combined into 52 sets, representing 18,980 days. The Maya had the most exact calendar ever developed in human history, and they were always revising it.

Threads

**To hold infinity in the palm of your hand
And eternity in an hour . . .**

Poet William Blake

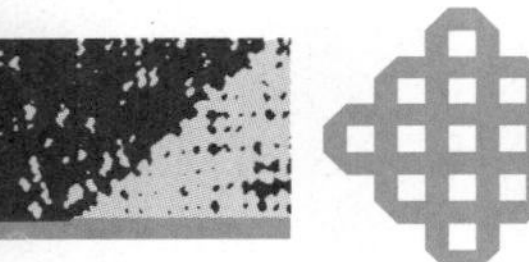

CULTURAL PATTERN 1: TWO CONCEPTS OF TIME

LEARNING STRATEGY

Forming Concepts: Breaking down a word into parts helps you understand the idea.

Task 2.3 Prereading

BREAKING DOWN A WORD

In the reading that comes next, you will see the words *monochronic* and *polychronic*.

Step 1. Look at the word *monochronic*. Break it into its two parts: *mono* (single, one) and *chronic* (from the Greek word *chronos,* or time). Putting the word back together, you have this meaning: "single time." What might this suggest to you? If you do not know, take a guess! Write your ideas in your notebook. Discuss them with someone else.

Step 2. Now consider the word *polychronic*. Divide it into two sections: *poly* and *chronic*. What do these parts mean? What does the whole word mean to you? Guess, if you do not know. Write your ideas in your notebook. Discuss them with someone else.

Task 2.4 Reading

LOOKING FOR NEW INFORMATION

Step 1. As you read, write down which cultures have M-time and which cultures have P-time.

Step 2. Note carefully the very helpful chart found toward the end of the reading.

Monochronic time (M-time) and polychronic time (P-time)

by Edward T. Hall and Mildred Reed Hall

There are many kinds of time systems in the world, but two are most important . . . . We call them monochronic and polychronic time. *Monochronic time* means paying attention to and doing only one thing at a time. *Polychronic time* means being involved with many things at once. Like oil and water, the two systems do not mix.

In monochronic cultures, time is experienced and used in a linear way—comparable to a road extending from the past into the future. Monochronic time is divided quite naturally into segments; it is scheduled and **compartmentalized,** making it possible for a person to concentrate on one thing at a time. In a monochronic system, the schedule may take **priority** above all else and be treated as sacred and unalterable.

Monochronic time is perceived as being almost **tangible:** people talk about it as though it were money, as something that can be "spent," "saved," "wasted," and "lost." It is also used as a classification system for ordering life and settling priorities: "I don't have time to see him." Because monochronic time concentrates on one thing at a time, people who are governed by it don't like to be **interrupted.** Monochronic time seals people off from one another and, as a result, **intensifies** some relationships while **shortchanging** others. Time becomes a room which some people are allowed to enter, while others are excluded.

Time chases people in M-cultures.

Monochronic time dominates most business in the United States. While Americans perceive it as almost in the air they breathe, it is nevertheless a learned product of northern European culture and is therefore **arbitrary** and imposed. Monochronic time is an artifact of the industrial revolution in England; factory life required the labor force to be on hand and in place at the appointed hour. In spite of the fact that it is *learned,* monochronic time now appears to be natural and logical because the great majority of Americans grew up in monochronic time systems with whistles and bells counting off the hours.

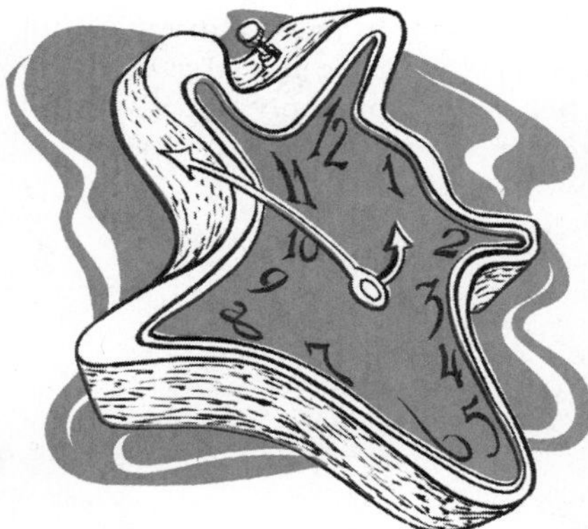

Time is flexible in P-cultures.

Other Western cultures—Switzerland, Germany, and Scandinavia in particular—are dominated by the iron hand of monochronic time as well. German and Swiss cultures represent classic examples of monochronic time. Still, monochronic time is not natural time; in fact, it seems to violate many of humanity's innate rhythms.

In almost every respect, polychronic systems are the **antithesis** of monochronic systems. Polychronic time is characterized by the simultaneous occurrence of many things and by a *great involvement with people.* There is more emphasis on completing human transactions than on holding to schedules. For example, two polychronic Latins conversing on a street corner would likely opt to be late for their next appointment rather than abruptly terminate the conversation before its natural conclusion. Polychronic time is experienced as much less tangible than monochronic time and can better be compared to a single point than to a road.

Proper understanding of the difference between monochronic and polychronic time systems will be helpful in dealing with the time-flexible Mediterranean [and Latin American] peoples. While the generalizations listed below do not apply equally to all cultures, they will help convey a pattern:

MONOCHRONIC PEOPLE	POLYCHRONIC PEOPLE
do one thing at a time	do many things at once
concentrate on the job	are highly distractible and subject to interruptions
take time **commitments** (deadlines, schedules) seriously	consider time commitments an objective to be achieved, if possible
are low-context and need information	are high-context and already have information
are committed to the job	are committed to people and human relationships
adhere religiously to plans	change plans often and easily
are concerned about not disturbing others; follow rules of **privacy** and consideration	are more concerned with those who are closely related (family, friends, close business associates) than with privacy
show great respect for private property; seldom borrow or lend	borrow and lend things often and easily
emphasize promptness	base promptness on the relationship
are **accustomed** to short-term relationships	have strong tendency to build lifetime relationships

Source: Edward T. Hall and Mildred Reed Hall, Understanding Cultural Differences, reprinted with permission of Intercultural Press, Inc., Yarmouth, Me. Copyright 1990, pp. 13–15.

Task 2.5 Postreading

WORKING WITH WORDS

Draw lines between any new words in the first column and their meanings in the second column. Guess if you need to. Go back and read the sentences using these words to find the context for guessing. (There are two extras in Column 2!)

COLUMN 1	COLUMN 2
monochronic	adapted to current conditions
compartmentalized	considerate, sensitive, caring
arbitrary	dealing with a concept of one-directional time
commitments	cheating or depriving
interrupted	strengthens
privacy	put into separate compartments or categories
accustomed	duties or agreements made for the future
tangible	not subject to rules, happening by whim
intensifies	freedom from intrusion
shortchanging	lifelong, permanent
polychronic	stopped in the middle of activity
	able to be valued or appraised
	concerning multidirectional time

Discussion questions: *Context* refers to informational background. What would high-context mean in a culture? Low-context?

LEARNING STRATEGY

Forming Concepts: Use proverbs to gain insight into a culture's values—but expect contradictions.

Task 2.6 Expanding Your Knowledge

CONSIDERING THE MEANING OF PROVERBS

Step 1. Every culture is rich with proverbs concerning time. Here are just a few proverbs from North American and Northern European cultures. Many of these have spread around the world to other English-speaking countries, such as India. In the blank, write down what each of the proverbs means. If you don't know, confer with someone else. Note that some proverbs contradict others.

a. "Time marches on." ______________________________

____

b. "Time heals all wounds." ______________________________

____

c. "Haste makes waste." ______________________________

____

d. "The early bird catches the worm." ______________________________

____

e. "Better late than never." ______________________________

____

f. "Make hay while the sun shines." ______________________________

____

g. "*Carpe diem* (seize the day)!" ______________________________

____

h. "A stitch in time saves nine." ______________________________

____

i. "Time and tide wait for no one." ______________________________

____

j. "A day late and a dollar short." ______________________________

____

Threads

Instant gratification takes too long.

Actress-writer Carrie Fisher

Step 2. Notice that most of the proverbs above urge us to move fast and accomplish things (M-time), while only a few deal with life *outside* of achievement or advancement (P-time). Write the letter M beside the proverbs that represent M-time and P beside those that represent P-time.

How many M's did you write? __________

How many P's did you write? __________

Step 3. Based on the results of Steps 1 and Step 2, describe in your notebook the culture of North America and Northern Europe concerning the concept of time.

Step 4. In your notebook, write down at least four proverbs that describe P-time. To do this, consult your classmates or look up proverbs in a book.

LEARNING STRATEGY

Forming Concepts: Drawing visual symbols can help you sharpen your understanding of cultural ideas.

Task 2.7 Prelistening

USING VISUAL SYMBOLS

On a large sheet of paper, draw symbols that represent M-time and P-time. (Examples: a wristwatch for M-time, a party scene for P-time.) Draw all the symbols you can for M-time and P-time. Be creative! Discuss your drawings with your classmates.

Task 2.8 Listening

LOOKING AT YOUR DRAWINGS

As you listen, look at the drawings of symbols of M-time and P-time. Let those visual symbols help you comprehend what you hear.

Your tape has **"More About M-Time and P-Time."** John Condon, *Good Neighbors: Communicating with the Mexicans,* reprinted with permission of Intercultural Press, Inc., Yarmouth, Me. Copyright 1985, pp. 65–66 [slightly adapted].

Task 2.9 Postlistening

MAKING A "TIME CONTINUUM"

Step 1. Place on a line the different cultures that Condon mentions. Start on the left with the culture that is loosest about time (P-cultures). On the right, place the cultures that are highly time conscious (M-cultures). In the middle, place the cultures that are in-between in their treatment of time. Try to put the cultures in their appropriate place in relation to each other's time values.

Step 2. Compare your line with the lines of others around you. Are they identical? If not, what are the differences and why did they emerge?

Threads

The space-time continuum—

Favorite theme of Star Trek

Task 2.10 Expanding Your Knowledge

SYNTHESIZING WHAT YOU KNOW IN A CONCEPT MAP OF MONOCHRONIC CULTURE

Step 1. On a separate sheet, make a list of all the *main* or *important* words that describe an M-culture, based on the information above. (Go back and listen to the tape again if you want. Review the chart in the reading passage if that helps.)

Step 2. Now draw a concept map of an M-culture. Be sure to include ideas like time commitments, schedule, compartmentalized, quiet, and so on.

IT WORKS! Learning Strategy: Making a Concept Map

EXAMPLE Put the phrase M-CULTURE in the middle and put a circle or oval around it. Now draw a line from the phrase M-CULTURE, and on or near that line

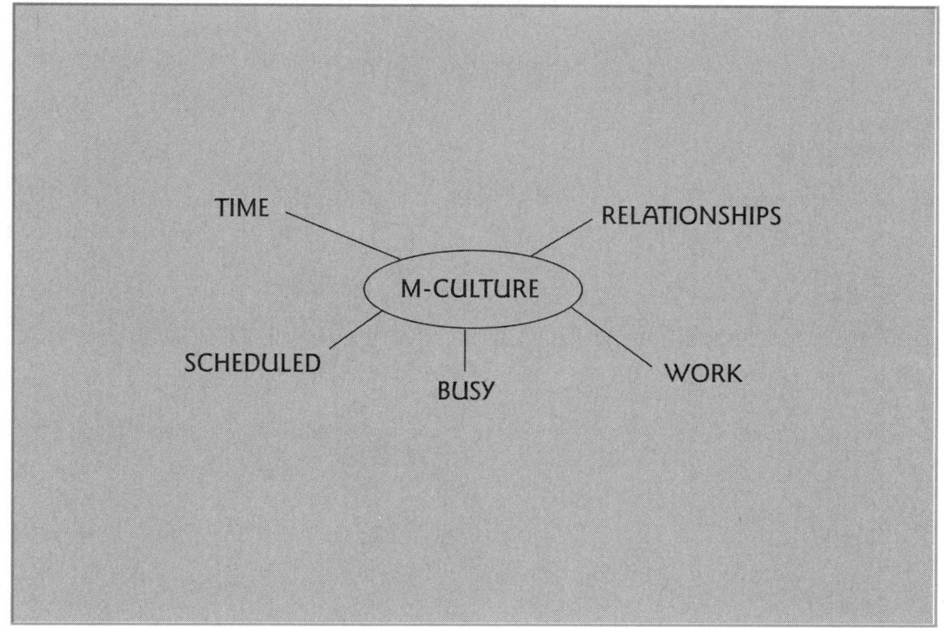

Concept map of an M-culture for you to complete.

write the word TIME. From the word TIME, draw lines and write words that indicate how this kind of culture deals with time (SCHEDULED, BUSY, and so on). Now make a line in any direction from the main circle or oval, and on or near that line write down the word WORK. From the word WORK put any number of lines describing how this culture treats work. Do the same with the word RELATIONSHIPS. Add as many other ideas and linkages you want.

Step 3. Compare your concept map with the maps of other people. Discuss similarities and differences.

Step 4. Add more ideas to your concept map now, if you want to.

Task 2.11 Expanding Your Knowledge

SYNTHESIZING WHAT YOU KNOW IN A CONCEPT MAP OF POLYCHRONIC CULTURES

Follow the steps in the task above to create a concept map describing P-cultures.

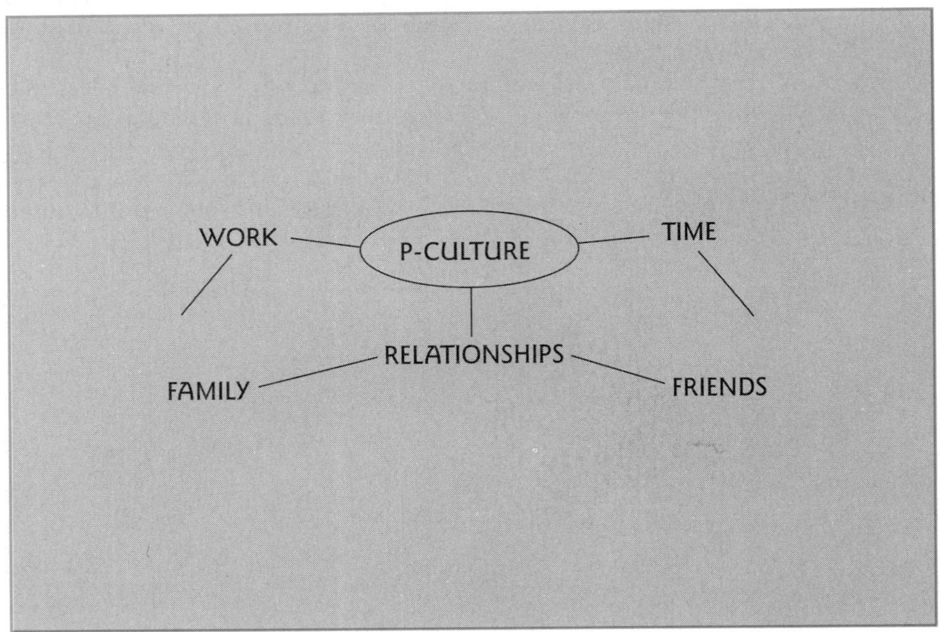

Concept map of a P-culture for you to complete.

CULTURAL PATTERN 2: BEHAVIOR IN TWO "TIME ZONES"

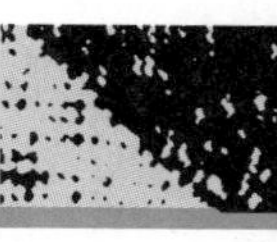

Task 2.12 Prereading

THINKING ABOUT WORKING MOTHERS

Step 1. In small groups, brainstorm all the tasks done by a *working mother* (in the West, that means a mother who has a paid job outside the home as well as a family at home).
Step 2. Compare lists across groups. Which group has the longest list?
Step 3. Discuss: Does the longest list reflect the reality, or are there still more tasks to add?

IT WORKS! Learning Strategy: Brainstorming

Betty

Threads

Had we but world enough and time . . .

Poet Andrew Marvell

LEARNING STRATEGY

Personalizing: Listening for personal details helps you understand the other person and her culture.

Task 2.13 Reading

LOOKING FOR DETAILS

Look for personal details as you read.

Keeping time

by Betty L.

My previous job was as dean of a government language school, where I received awards for training teachers to teach more effectively and for speeding up students' learning, so that they reached their language goals more rapidly.

A year ago I started an international company. I spent months assembling the board of directors, designing brochures, organizing courses and programs, writing dozens of proposals for funds, and conducting programs in the U.S. and Russia. During this time, some Russian immigrants came to stay at my house; fortunately, these visitors helped a lot at home and made life easier. At the same time, I wrote several books to be published by my company and co-edited a book for a major publisher. I'm grateful I have a photographic memory, so I can remember everything I see; otherwise, my productivity might be slowed down.

In addition to my work, I have a family at home, including a husband and children. Some of the children have had serious health problems from birth, but I try to handle those problems well and efficiently. With tremendous cooperation from my husband and with help from the kids themselves, the kids are fed and clothed and educated.

I am busy from the time I get up until the time I go to bed. My time has to be carefully planned. I do not like to be interrupted, because I want to accomplish my goals. I keep a sense of humor about it all, even when I'm madly finishing the last draft of a brochure or book, driving one of the kids to the doctor, or talking on the phone about business plans. I never get "burned out" because I like what I do.

Source: From an interview of Betty L.
by Rebecca L. Oxford.
Used with permission.

Task 2.14 Postreading

GETTING TO KNOW BETTY

Write your answers in your notebook, then discuss them with others.

Step 1. What does Betty do for a living now?
Step 2. What are some of the tasks she does in this job?
Step 3. What was her job before this?
Step 4. Describe Betty's family.
Step 5. What good things does Betty do for her family?
Step 6. Would you call Betty a workaholic? Why or why not? Are workaholics frequently found in M-culture? Would Betty agree with author Diane Fassel (*Working Ourselves to Death: The High Cost of Workaholism, the Rewards of Recovery,* San Francisco: Harper & Row, 1990, p. 10) in the following statement? "Inevitably, if workaholism is not interrupted, people burn out." Explain your answer.

Task 2.15 Expanding Your Knowledge

CONSIDERING PEOPLE YOU KNOW FROM M-CULTURES

Step 1. In your notebook, write down the names of people that you know who are a little like Betty or who fit the descriptions of people who live in M-cultures. Most of us have encountered at least one or more such individuals.

Step 2. Is your list long or short?

Step 3. Do you know many people who are from M-cultures or who use M-type behavior in their lives? Why or why not?

Step 4. In your notebook, make two columns. List the advantages and disadvantages these people have.

Step 5. Discuss your results with someone else and compare.

Task 2.16 Prelistening

CONSIDERING A KEY WORD

The word *priorities* means things that come first in order of importance. What would be among the top priorities in a P-culture? List them in your notebook.

Your tape has **"I Know My Priorities,"** by Jorge V. (interviewed by Rebecca L. Oxford). Used with permission.

Task 2.17 Listening

PRIORITIZING

As you listen, write down Jorge's priorities. Be as specific as you can. (Don't just write "work" or "family.")

Jorge, family, and friends

Task 2.18 Postlistening

UNDERSTANDING JORGE

Step 1. In what country does Jorge live?
Step 2. How far is his house from his mother's house?
Step 3. Why does he visit his mother's house each day?
Step 4. What kind of job does Jorge have?
Step 5. What new job does he want?
Step 6. What is his attitude about work?
Step 7. What is his attitude about family?
Step 8. Which is more important to him, work or family?
Step 9. Based on the story and on your own opinion, will Jorge ever fix his resume for the new job? Explain.
Step 10. Would you like Jorge as your friend? Explain.
Step 11. How would you feel if you were Jorge's working partner? Explain.
Step 12. What makes Jorge a good example of P-culture?
Step 13. Discuss your ideas with someone else.

Task 2.19 Expanding Your Knowledge

CONSIDERING PEOPLE YOU KNOW FROM P-CULTURES

Step 1. In your notebook, write down the names of people that you know who are something like Jorge or who fit the descriptions of people who live in P-cultures. Most of us know at least one or more individuals like this.
Step 2. Is your list long or short?
Step 3. Do you know many people who are from P-cultures or who use P-type behavior in their lives? Explain.
Step 4. In your notebook, make two columns. List the advantages and disadvantages these people have.
Step 5. Discuss your results with someone else and compare.

All boxed in: time in M-cultures

Doonesbury BY GARRY TRUDEAU

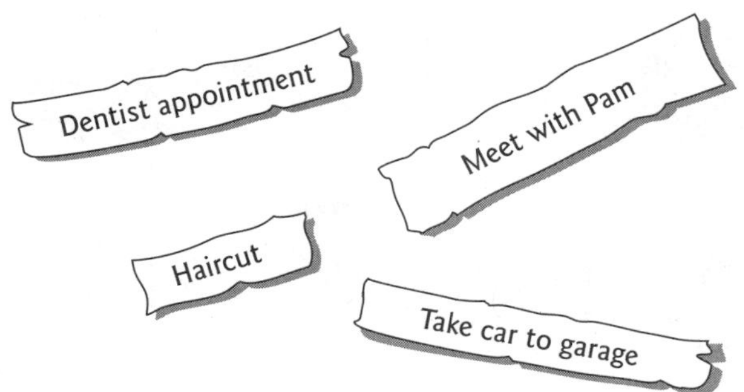

Light as air: time in P-cultures

Time waits for no one.

Task 2.20 Expanding Your Knowledge

THINKING ABOUT TIME IN OTHER CULTURES

Step 1. Discuss: Besides the countries noted in this chapter, what countries do you know that might be considered M-cultures? What countries do you know that might be called P-cultures?

Step 2. Explain why you have categorized them in this way.

Task 2.21 Expanding Your Knowledge

DOING A "TIME" ROLE-PLAY

Create a role-play of a conflict between a person from an M-culture and a person from a P-culture.

Step 1. To do this, first make "role-cards" for each person. On the role-cards, make notes of how each person might think, feel, believe, or act concerning time, work, information, relationships, and so on.

Step 2. Give the role cards to individuals who will act out the roles. As they act out the roles, see how the aggravation and frustration builds between people with M and P ways of behaving.

Step 3. During or after the role-play, find some ways to resolve the differences.

Step 4. After this, discuss the role-play as a whole and take notes on what you have learned.

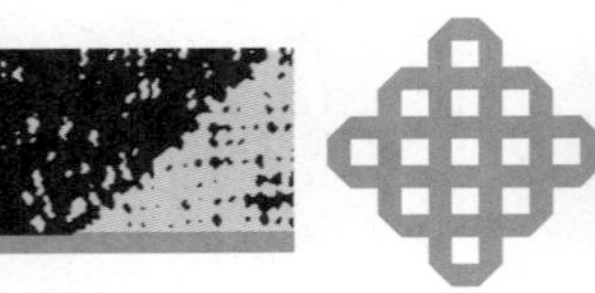

CULTURAL PATTERN 3: THE CONNECTION OF TIME AND SPACE: TWO PERSPECTIVES

Task 2.22 Prereading

PREDICTING THE KIND OF WRITING

IT WORKS! Learning Strategy: Predicting

One of the following short perspectives is from science fiction, and the other is from the science of anthropology. What differences would you expect in the content (what is said about time) or in style (how the writer says it) of these two perspectives?

Task 2.23 Reading

LOOKING FOR DIFFERENCES IN CONTENT AND STYLE

As you read the two perspectives, compare them for content (what is said concerning time) and style (how it is said). After the reading, you will make a chart about this.

A science fiction view of time and space

by Sheri S. Tepper

Everything, so says Jordel of Hemerlane, is connected to everything else. Time imposes no limitation on this rule. Everywhen is connected to every-other-when. Tit floweth from tat, tut floweth from tit. Past, present, future are not disparate things but a continuum, a recoiled **helix** of interconnections in which time no more serves to sever than distance. Here and now are not separable. Now and then are not divisible. Everything burrows through the **myriad wormholes** of reality to become part of everything else. Time and space are coiled like some unimaginable DNA, pregnant with both possibility and certainty. In this multidimensional womb, separation is a fiction, all things are adjacent, and twentieth-century Earth snuggles close against the warm cheeks of the planet Elsewhere . . . .

Source: From SIDESHOW by Sheri S. Tepper. Copyright 1993. Used by permission of Bantam Books, a division of Bantam Doubleday Dell Publishing Group, Inc.

A scientific view of time and space

by Edward T. Hall
and Mildred Reed Hall

In monochronic time cultures the emphasis is on the compartmentalization of functions and people. Private offices are soundproof if possible. In polychronic mediterranean cultures, business offices often have large reception areas where people can wait. Company and government officials may even transact their business by moving about in the reception area, stopping to confer with this group and that one until everyone has been attended to.

Polychronic people feel that private space disrupts the flow of information by shutting people off from one another. In polychronic systems, appointments mean very little and may be shifted around even at the last minute to accommodate someone more important in an individual's hierarchy of family, friends, or associates. Some polychronic people (such as Latin Americans and Arabs) give precedence to their large circle of family members over any business obligation. Polychronic people also have many close friends and good clients with whom they spend a great deal of time. The close links to clients or customers create a reciprocal feeling of obligation and a mutual desire to be helpful.

Source: Edward T. Hall and Mildred Reed Hall, Understanding Cultural Differences, reprinted with permission of Intercultural Press, Inc., Yarmouth, Me. Copyright 1990, pp. 15–16.

LEARNING STRATEGY

Forming Concepts: Making a chart enables you to analyze information efficiently.

Task 2.24 Postreading

COMPARING TWO PERSPECTIVES AFTER THE READING

Make a chart of content and style, and complete it. The chart might look like the following one.

CHART OF SCIENCE FICTION AND SCIENCE VIEWS OF TIME AND SPACE

	SCIENCE FICTION (TEPPER)	SCIENCE (HALL AND HALL)
CONTENT	______	______
(What is said)	______	______
STYLE	______	______
(How it is said)	______	______

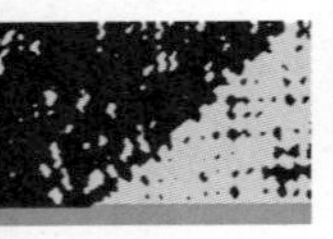

CULTURAL PATTERN 4: YOUR OWN TERRITORY AND SPACE

Task 2.25 Prelistening

THINKING ABOUT THE BUBBLE

Discuss with others: What do you think personal space might be? How can personal space be like an invisible bubble around you? Who gets into the bubble, and who is left outside?

Task 2.26 Listening

LISTEN FOR THE IMAGES

As you listen, recognize that you can actually "see" images or pictures while you are hearing about them. Use your "mind's eye" to see every image, such as the bubble, the way people stand too close, etc.

LEARNING STRATEGY

Remembering New Material: Using mental images helps you remember new material that you hear (or read).

Your tape has "**Territory and Personal Space**" by Edward T. Hall and Mildred Reed Hall. *Understanding Cultural Differences,* reprinted with permission of Intercultural Press, Inc., Yarmouth, Me. Copyright 1990, pp. 10–12.

Closed spaces in the city

Task 2.27 Postlistening

ANALYZING WHAT YOU HEARD

Step 1. How many images did you "see" while listening? What were they?
Step 2. How can images help you understand and remember?
Step 3. Have you ever felt that someone was crowding you by standing too close? If so, describe the situation.
Step 4. Have you ever felt someone was acting aloof by standing too far away for normal conversation? If so, describe the situation.
Step 5. Have you ever thought it was strange when you visited a house and all the doors to the inside rooms were closed? If so, describe the situation.
Step 6. Have you been taken on a tour of someone's home and been shown rooms that you thought were too private to display? If so, describe the situation.
Step 7. Discuss your answers with at least one other person.

Task 2.28 Prereading

STANDING NEAR AND FAR

Before doing the reading, in a small group practice standing first near one another and then farther away. Discuss: What distances seem to be most comfortable, and why?

LEARNING STRATEGY

Forming Concepts: Making a numbered diagram of space (or other cultural concepts) can help you understand cultural differences.

Task 2.29 Reading

DRAWING A DIAGRAM

As you read, draw a one-page diagram indicating the most typical North American "comfort zones" for the following: intimate distance, social distance, and public distance. Be sure to give the numbers in feet and/or inches.

Other kinds of space in North American culture: intimate, social, and public

by Julius Fast

Intimate Distance

Intimate distance can either be *close,* that is, actual contact, or *far,* from 6 to 18 inches. The close phase of intimate distance is used for making love, for very close friendships, and for children clinging to a parent or to each other.

When you are at *close* intimate distance, you are overwhelmingly aware of your partner . . . . It is most natural between a man and a woman on intimate terms . . . . Between two women in our culture, a close intimate state is acceptable, while in some Arab cultures such a state is acceptable between two men. Men will frequently walk hand in hand in certain Arab countries and in many Mediterranean lands. [See Chapter 3 for cultural rules about touching.]

The *far* phase of intimate distance is still close enough to clasp hands, but it is not considered an acceptable distance for two adult male Americans [unless they are homosexual]. When a subway or an elevator brings them into such crowded circumstances, they will automatically observe rigid rules of behavior, such as standing stiffly, looking away, and not touching . . . .

Social Distance

Social distance too has a close phase and a far phase. The *close* phase is four to seven feet and is generally the distance at which we transact impersonal business. It is the distance we assume when, in business, we meet the client from out of town, the new art director, or the office manager. It is the distance the housewife keeps from the repairman, the shop clerk, or the delivery boy . . . . The boss utilizes this distance to dominate a seated employee—a secretary or receptionist. To the employee, he or she tends to loom above and gain height and strength . . . .

The *far* phase of social distance, seven to 12 feet, is for more formal social or business relationships. The "big boss" will have a desk large enough to put him or her this distance from the employees. The boss can also remain seated at this distance and look up at an employee without a loss of status . . . . At this distance, it is not proper to look briefly and look away. The only contact you have is visual, so tradition dictates that you hold the person's eyes during conversation. This distance allows a certain protection. You can keep working at this distance and not be rude, or you can stop working and talk. In offices it is necessary to preserve this far social distance between the receptionist and the visitor so that the receptionist may continue working without having to chat with the visitor. A closer distance would make such an action rude.

The husband and wife at home in the evening assume this far social distance to relax. They can talk to each other if they wish or simply read instead of talking. The impersonal air of this type of social distance makes it an almost mandatory thing when a large family lives together, but often the family is arranged for this polite separation and must be pulled more closely together for a more intimate evening.

Public Distance

Finally, *public* distance is the farthest extension of our territorial bondage. Again there is a close phase and a far phase . . . . The *close* phase of public distance is 12 to 25 feet, and this is suited for more informal gatherings, such as a teacher's address in a roomful of students, or a boss at a conference of workers. The *far* phase of public distance, 25 feet or more, is generally reserved for politicians where the distance is also a safety or a security factor, as it is with animals. Certain animal species will let you come only within this distance before moving away.

Task 2.30 Postreading

COMPARING ACROSS CULTURES

Step 1. Are the distances (intimate, social, and public) the same or different across cultures? Give examples.

Step 2. Where you come from, is it appropriate for men to touch within intimate distance? Explain.

Step 3. What would be the reaction(s) of a woman if a man moves into her intimate space? How might this differ across cultures?

Step 4. Domination by the boss in social space is a purely cultural concept. Does it exist in your culture? Why or why not?

Step 5. Do you think all or most North American husbands and wives keep a far social distance when relaxing at home in the evening? Circle one: YES or NO. Explain why or why not.

Step 6. Why do you think the author mentioned animals in the discussion of public space?

Task 2.31 Prelistening

CONSIDERING THE CLICHES

Consider clichés (worn out, common phrases) like the "wide open spaces" and the "wild West." What do these clichés tell you about space in the United States? Discuss them with others.

Task 2.32 Listening

SEPARATING THE SERIOUS FROM THE FUNNY

Listen for the serious comments about space as well as the humorous comments. Which ones are which? How can you tell?

Your tape has **"Space in the U.S."**

The bubble of personal space in the United States is two to four feet.

Minimum acceptable distance between parent and teenager in public

COLORADO	KANSAS
Denver	Wichita

Task 2.33 Postlistening

UNDERSTANDING SPACE

Step 1. In your opinion, why do families in the United States move so often?
Step 2. Is frequent moving a good thing? Why or why not?
Step 3. Do teenagers in other cultures want to stay as far as possible from their parents? Why or why not?
Step 4. How do you feel about the traditional U.S. home? Why?
Step 5. Do you like the nontraditional U.S. home better or not? Why?
Step 6. Which kind of U.S. home would you rather visit? Explain why.
Step 7. Compare your answers with those of other people.

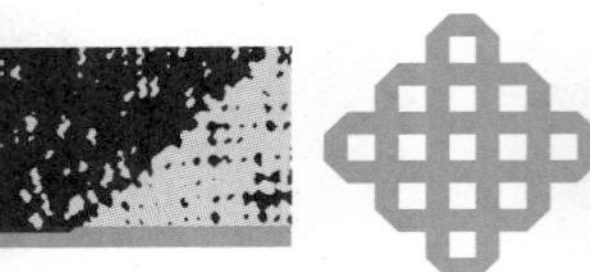

CULTURAL PATTERN 5: SPACE IN OTHER PARTS OF THE WORLD

Task 2.34 Prereading

ASKING QUESTIONS

Read the title of the piece. The title contains the phrase "sacred space." Why would space be "sacred" in Germany and other Northern European countries? What does *sacred* mean here? What does that suggest to you about what you will read?

LEARNING STRATEGY

Testing Hypotheses: Search for evidence to test your hypotheses, and revise those hypotheses if necessary.

Task 2.35 Reading

LOCATING EVIDENCE

Write down or underline each time you find *evidence* of the sacredness of space in the countries mentioned.

Sacred space in Germany and other northern European countries

Space is sacred in Germany. The standing distance (personal space) is greater in Germany than in the United States. Unlike people in the United States, the Germans are not very mobile; they do not move every few years. However, like people in the United States, Germans feel that their home is their castle.

The German concept of self requires a wide area of privacy, which is often formal and regimented. Doors, hedges, fences: these physical features of a German home reflect an emphasis on privacy, which is pervasive throughout German life. The sense of privacy is reflected not just in a house but also in a small apartment. In German houses, doors are firmly shut between rooms to suggest the need for personal space and individual privacy. The ideal German house has a entrance hall that leads visitors into the house without showing specific rooms and spoiling the family's privacy. It is an honor to be invited into a German home; this does not frequently happen to foreigners, who are usually viewed with suspicion. Pieces of furniture are heavy and placed far apart, so that personal space is maintained during conversation. Formal interactions—not relaxed, happy-go-lucky conversations—are common. Heavy drapes prevent prying eyes from the outside from seeing in.

Good German neighbors are quiet, do not intrude, keep the sidewalk clean, and tend the flowers nicely. They do not "drop by for a chat." Leases often say who can use the garden or yard and at which hours and who will sweep stairwell and sidewalk. Time periods for noise (even running water) are often prescribed. Sometimes Germans are not allowed to use their running water after ten o'clock at night! The formality of personal space and social distance is maintained by outside doors that are split, opening only at waist height. The outdoors are very important to Germans. Gardens, lawns, and balconies are used often for dining as well as for gardening; these are made as private as possible. It is possible to live in the same German neighborhood for years without having a relationship with one's neighbors.

Germany is similar to many other northern European countries, including Scandinavian countries and England. In these countries, people living next to each other are not necessarily expected to interact unless they have already met socially. In northern Europe in general, personal space is quite large, and people remain at a distance. They do not ordinarily touch each other unless they know each other very well. "Dropping in" is simply not an option; you are considered very rude if you do not call in advance to arrange a visit in countries like England, Belgium, Luxembourg, Finland, Norway, and Denmark. Even in Austria, where there is a customary visiting hour at 3:00 PM, you still must call in advance. Only in certain countries (Sweden is an example) can you drop in

Doors, hedges, and fences create German privacy.

Saunas: a northern European surprise in the realm of personal space

unannounced—and this can occur just in the countryside or at summer homes, never in the city. In most of these northern European countries, don't expect the grand tour of the host's home. Unlike the informality and openness found in the United States, northern European privacy dictates that you will not get to see most of the rooms of the house.

However, a big **paradox** exists in at least two Scandinavian countries, Finland and Denmark. Personal space and family privacy are indeed crucial there. Yet people who live in these two countries often go to the sauna (pronounced "sow-na"), a small wooden house with a main room where bathers—usually naked—sit or lie on wooden shelves. Among total strangers, acquaintances, or good friends, people steam themselves with heat from rocks on top of a small stove, not worrying at all about their nudity. In fact, many business discussions are held in saunas. After the sauna, people often hit each other with birch leaves to improve their blood circulation. Then they dive into a cold lake or pool, roll in the snow, or take a shower. The sauna is usually segregated by sex, with men in one and women in another; or men and women can alternate in the same sauna. Sometimes whole families or good friends of the opposite sex take saunas together. A caution: saunas are not designed to stimulate the sex drive. The sauna philosophy says that contemplation and health are the result of saunas, and that people should act in saunas as they would in places of worship. Thus, the sauna—which at first might seem to strip people of their privacy entirely—has a mystique of worshipfulness and quiet that might actually protect privacy.

Source: Contains some concepts from John C. Condon and Fathi Yousef, "Out of House and Home," in Louise F. Luce and Elise C. Smith (eds.), Toward Internationalism: Readings in Cross-Cultural Communication, pp. 99–116, Cambridge, Mass.: Newbury House/Harper & Row, 1977; and some also from Nancy L. Braganti and Elizabeth Devine, European Customs and Manners, New York: Simon & Schuster, 1992.

LEARNING STRATEGY

Forming Concepts: To expand your understanding, first summarize the reading and then go beyond the summary with your imagination.

Task 2.36 Postreading

EXPLORING THE READING AND GOING FURTHER

Step 1. In your own words, write down five characteristics of a German house that ensure privacy.

____

____

____

____

____

Threads

A journey of a thousand li begins with a single step.

Asian proverb

Step 2. What should good German neighbors do, according to the reading? List at least three things.

____

____

____

Step 3. Imagine other things that good German neighbors should do that were *not* mentioned in the reading. List at least three things.

____

____

Step 4. Why is it a paradox or contradiction that some northern Europeans like to use saunas but still want personal space and privacy? How do you explain this? Write your responses.

____

____

Step 5. The reading says that Germans and most other northern Europeans like a lot of personal space. Why do you think this occurs? How do you react to this? Write two or three paragraphs on a separate sheet expressing your ideas and personal reactions.

Step 6. Discuss your answers to Steps 1 through 5 with someone else.

Task 2.37 Prelistening

PREDICTING WHAT'S COMING

IT WORKS!
Learning Strategy:
Predicting

You have already discovered that personal space is large in Northern Europe. Discuss with others: What about space in Southern Europe (the Mediterranean area) and Latin America? Would you predict that the size of personal Mediterranean and Latin American space would be small or large? Why?

LEARNING STRATEGY

Managing Your Learning: After you have made a prediction, check yourself to see if you were right.

Task 2.38 Listening

CHECKING YOURSELF

You have already made a prediction about personal space in Mediterranean and Latin American areas. As you listen, check to see whether your prediction was right. Ask yourself why or why not.

Your tape has "**Mediterranean and Latin American Space.**"

Task 2.39 Postlistening

EXPLAINING ABOUT PERSONAL SPACE

Step 1. Spain, Italy, and France are located close to each other, and these cultures require very little personal space between people. How can these three cultures, which have so much in common regarding personal space, have such different ideas about family privacy?

Step 2. Using your own judgment, list these three countries (France, Spain, Italy) according to their needs for privacy at home.

Most private: ______________________________

Second most private: ______________________________

Least private: ______________________________

Step 3. In which of the countries would you most like to visit a home as a guest? Explain.

Step 4. In which home would you be most comfortable just coming by without calling? Explain.

Step 5. Are your answers to Steps 1–4 the same as those of other people? Compare and contrast your answers in a discussion.

LEARNING STRATEGY

Forming Concepts: Form concepts quickly by reading the first sentence of each paragraph in the story.

Task 2.40 Prereading

SKIMMING WITH FIRST SENTENCES

Skim through the following reading by looking at the first sentence of each paragraph (which is usually the topic sentence). What are the three main ideas of this piece, based on your skimming?

Task 2.41 Reading

PAYING CAREFUL ATTENTION

Now that you have skimmed the piece, read it more carefully, paying attention to the small details.

My son and I discover Latin space

by Maury M. Breecher

My son Michael and I have come to Latin America to study Spanish at a language institute. We are living with a local family in a middle-class home. I have lots of work to do with my studies, translating Spanish stories and articles day after day.

My 16-year-old son takes his studying less seriously and is just having fun. Michael thinks he is God's gift to Latin women, and Latin women seem to think so, too! He is constantly surrounded by teenage girls who want to "practice their English" with him.

In a typical day in our new home, at least six to ten visitors drop in, usually unannounced. Among these are relatives and friends of all family members, plus the chauffeur who comes in an old battered Mercedes (a sign of better economic times) to pick me up for tutoring sessions and for tours around town. I am astounded by the sheer amount of socializing in this house from midday through late at night.

The phone rings incessantly. It is found in the TV room, which is something like a small den just off the large main living room (which no one uses because it is too formal). While five or more people are crammed into the small space watching TV, Michael or one of the family members sits on the phone for hours chatting with friends.

In this house, we have found that our personal space is smaller than it ever was in North America. People stand very close when talking with us, and we know it is impolite to back away. Everyone is very friendly and physical, even though we are foreigners and they don't know us well yet. Being from another country seems to be okay here, sometimes even a conversation-starter with people who drop by the house or with others whom Michael and I meet on the street or at the institute.

We are starting to do things the Latin way ourselves. We now use very warm, physical greetings, often kissing and hugging the people in the house. We talk loudly and shout from room to room to get messages across, just like our hosts do. We are not surprised if someone walks into one of our rooms to sit down and have a personal chat, or if someone "borrows" one of our rooms to have a private talk with someone else. Like our hosts, we freely lend things and ask for what we need. The distance of the U.S. has evaporated, even though there is still some formality in addressing older people.

We find the same situation about space at the institute. There is a lot of background noise (city traffic, airplanes flying overhead, four thousand students studying in one building) to intrude on our territory. People stand very close to each other and talk loudly during coffee breaks, which take place in the hallways even if classes are going on inside some of the classrooms right next to the hall. Girls often hold hands, and boys sometimes put arms around each other's shoulders as they walk. Students consider their social life as important as their learning. To us, the new experience in small personal space is pleasant and friendly—most of the time.

Maury and Michael in Latin America

Task 2.42 Postreading

GIVING YOUR VIEWS AND FEELINGS

Step 1. Decide whether you would like to live in the home described above. Explain.

Step 2. Decide whether you would like to go to an institute like the one mentioned above. Explain.

Step 3. What does Michael like to do in this new culture?

Step 4. What is Maury's goal in this new culture?

Step 5. Is Maury's goal similar to your goal? Why or why not?

Step 6. Do you think Michael's and Maury's goals might ever conflict while they are living in the new culture? Explain.

Step 7. Share your personal views with someone else and compare.

Task 2.43 Prelistening

CONSIDERING WHAT YOU ALREADY KNOW

As you can tell from the title, the piece discusses space in Japan and some Arabic-speaking countries. What do you already know about space in Japan? About space in Arabic-speaking countries?

Task 2.44 Listening

LOOKING FOR NEW INFORMATION

As you listen, try to find new information beyond what you already know. Take notes in a T-line chart, with Japan on one side and Arabic-speaking countries on the other. Your chart might look like the following.

SPACE IN DIFFERENT COUNTRIES

JAPAN	SOME ARABIC-SPEAKING COUNTRIES

Your tape has **"Space in Japan and Some Arabic-Speaking Countries."** From *BODY LANGUAGE*. Copyright © 1970 by Julius Fast. Reprinted by permission of the publisher, M. Evans and Company, Inc. [slightly adapted].

Task 2.45 Postlistening

CONSIDERING THE CONTRASTS

Step 1. Why do people in the countries mentioned above cling to one another?

Step 2. What are the similarities between the Japanese and the Arabic-speaking people in terms of their concept of space?
Step 3. What are the differences?
Step 4. How might someone from North America or Northern Europe react to the Japanese and Arab concepts of space?
Step 5. How do you react to the Japanese and Arab concepts of space?

Task 2.46 Expanding Your Knowledge

JUDGING YOUR PREFERRED PERSONAL SPACE

Discuss with one other person:

Step 1. What amount of distance between two good friends seems just right to you?
Step 2. How much space should be left between two new acquaintances? Between two strangers?
Step 3. Why do you have these opinions? How does your culture affect your feelings about personal space?
Step 4. Does your culture encourage small personal space or large personal space?

Task 2.47 Expanding Your Knowledge

UNDERSTANDING THE BACKING-OFF SYNDROME

Step 1. Imagine this: While you are talking with an acquaintance from the United States, you see that he or she keeps stepping backward as if to move away from you.
Step 2. Do you think the person is rude or uneducated?
Step 3. Do you think the person dislikes you?
Step 4. Do you think the person is prejudiced against people from your culture and does not want to be around them?
Step 5. Do you think the person needs more personal space than you do?
Step 6. What other possibilities exist? Which one seems the most reasonable? Why?
Step 7. Discuss your ideas with someone else or write them down in your notebook.

Task 2.48 Expanding Your Knowledge

PLAYING ROLES ABOUT PERSONAL SPACE

Conduct a role-play in which people play individuals from Germany, France, Italy, Spain, England, the Middle East, and Japan. (It would be great to have people who are really from those countries to play themselves!) In the role-play, everyone will visit the home of the person from Germany and will respond and react as representatives of the cultures they have been assigned for the role-play (France, Italy, and so on).

Step 1. Before the role-play, discuss: How would people from these different cultures react when visiting a German home? Would they be comfortable? What might they want to see or do? What might the German host want to happen?
Step 2. Conduct the role-play.
Step 3. After the role-play, take five or ten minutes to discuss what happened and how people reacted.

Alternative: You can also rotate the cultures of the hosts. Try having a person play the role of a host from the Middle East or Japan or one of the other cultures.

Task 2.49 Expanding Your Knowledge

INTERVIEWING SOMEONE ABOUT PERSONAL SPACE

Step 1. Interview a friend or colleague who has been in a culture that emphasizes large personal space. Ask whether the person's home culture also demands personal space. If not, did the person feel threatened, confused, unhappy, or hurt (or possibly relieved?) in the culture that has large personal space?
Step 2. Now interview someone who has visited or lived in a culture with small personal space. Find out whether the person's native culture also has small personal space. If not, how did the person feel (crowded, angry, upset, etc.)?

Task 2.50 Expanding Your Knowledge

TAKING A FIELD TRIP TO ANOTHER PART OF TOWN

Step 1. Go to a part of the town or city that has a different sense of personal space, if possible. This might be an ethnic location where there are shops, restaurants, or places of worship that come from another culture.
Step 2. Determine how close the personal space is. To do this, walk around and see how close together people stand.
Step 3. Find out whether friendliness and verbal greetings are in any way related to personal space in this setting.
Step 4. Determine how you feel in a situation where the amount of personal space is different from that with which you are familiar.
Step 5. Discuss your feelings and observations with your friends.

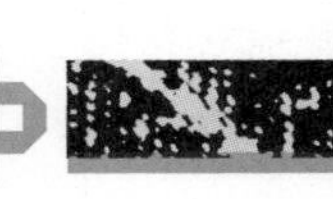

LEARNING STRATEGY

Managing Your Learning: Find a useful way to organize the new vocabulary so that you can learn it easily.

Task 2.51 Wordbuilding

ORGANIZING THE NEW VOCABULARY

In this chapter some words were marked that may be new to you. Organize these in any way that you would like: in your notebook, on flashcards, on colored slips of paper—whatever helps you learn them most easily.

accustomed—adapted to existing conditions
antithesis—the direct opposite
arbitrary—decided by chance or whim, not by rule
boarders—people who receive board (meals) and a room in exchange for payment of some kind
brass—the most important people, those who wear the brass
commitments—agreements or pledges to do something in the future
compartmentalized—separated into isolated compartments or categories
gastronomic—dealing with culinary (food) customs or style
helix—spiral
indolence—laziness
intensifies—increases in density, strengthens
interrupted—stopped in the middle of something
mañana—tomorrow (in Spanish)
monochronic—single duration
myriad—a great number
paradox—contradiction
polychronic—multiple duration
priority—precedence in date or importance
privacy—freedom from undesirable interruptions or intrusions
shortchanging—cheating or depriving
subordinates—people of lesser rank or position
tangible—capable of being appraised at an actual or approximate value
taskmaster—one who imposes work on another
wormhole—a hole burrowed by worms; in science fiction, a shortcut between two quadrants in space

CHECKING YOUR SUCCESS

Task 2.52 Evaluating

REVIEWING THE OBJECTIVES AND RATING YOURSELF

Circle YES or NO below.

Can you . . .

• describe two cultural modes of looking at time?	YES	NO
• explain why cultures look at time differently?	YES	NO
• discuss how different concepts of time influence relationships and work?	YES	NO
• explain the concept of personal space?	YES	NO
• describe cultural differences in space?	YES	NO
• use many new learning strategies to make your studying easier?	YES	NO

WHERE TO GO FOR MORE INFORMATION

Barry, Dave (1991). *Dave Barry's only travel guide you'll ever need.* New York: Fawcett Columbine.

Braganti, Nancy L., & Elizabeth Devine (1992). *European customs and manners.* New York: Simon & Schuster.

Condon, John C. (1985). *Good neighbors: Communicating with the Mexicans.* Yarmouth, Me.: Intercultural Press.

Condon, John C., & Fathi Yousef (1987). Out of house and home. In Louise F. Luce & Elise C. Smith (eds.), *Toward internationalism: Readings in cross-cultural communication* (pp. 99–116). Cambridge, Mass.: Newbury House/Harper & Row. Now Boston: Heinle & Heinle.

Fassel, Diane (1990). *Working ourselves to death: The high cost of workaholism and the rewards of recovery.* San Francisco: Harper San Francisco.

Fulghum, Robert. *It was on fire when I lay down on it.* New York: Ivy/Ballentine, 1989.

Gallagher, Winifred (1989, Apr.). Success. *American Health,* 55.

Gibbs, Nancy (1989, Apr. 24). How America has run out of time. *Time,* 61.

Hall, Edward T. (1976). *Beyond culture.* New York: Doubleday.

Hall, Edward T. (1969). *The hidden dimension.* New York: Doubleday.

Hall, Edward T., & Mildred Reed Hall (1990). *Understanding different cultures.* Yarmouth, Me.: Intercultural Press.

Moon, William Least Heat (1982). *Blue highways: A journey into America.* New York: Fawcett Crest.

Morain, Genelle G. (1987). Kinesics and cross-cultural understanding. In Louise F. Luce & Elise C. Smith (eds.), *Toward internationalism: Readings in cross-cultural communication* (pp. 117–142). Cambridge, Mass.: Newbury House/Harper & Row. Now Boston: Heinle & Heinle.

Neikirk, John O. (1988, Aug./Sept.). Workaholism: The pain others applaud. *Focus Magazine,* 1.

Peterson, Karen S. (1993, Aug. 27). Work fiends turn a cold shoulder on chilling out. *USA Today,* p. 4D.

Robinson, Bryan (1992). *Overdoing it: How to slow down and take care of yourself.* Deerfield Beach, Fla.: Health Communications.

Schaef, Anne Wilson, & Diane Fassel (1988). *The addictive organization.* San Francisco: Harper San Francisco.

Stewart, Edward C., & Milton J. Bennett (1991). *American cultural patterns: A cross-cultural perspective.* Yarmouth, Me.: Intercultural Press.

Yates, Ronald (1988, Nov. 13). Japanese live . . . and die . . . for their work. *Chicago Tribune,* p. 1.

Let's Get Physical

3

CHAPTER

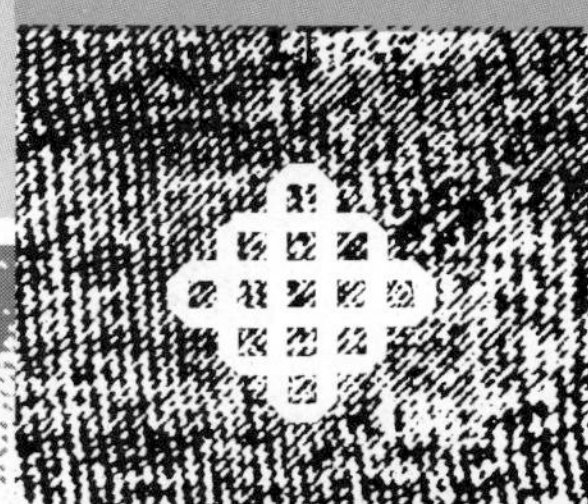

INTRODUCTION

PREVIEW QUESTIONS

1. Why is nonverbal communication so important?
2. What cultural differences exist in touch?
3. What do different types of gestures mean?
4. What does posture tell us?
5. What meanings do different **gazes*** convey?

Actions speak louder than words.

—*Proverb*

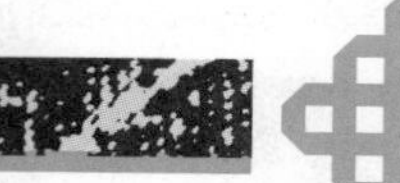

PATTERNS IN THIS CHAPTER

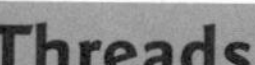

Threads

I want to hold your hand.

The Beatles

This chapter deals with four cultural patterns, all of them nonverbal: touch, gesture, posture, and gaze. Nonverbal communication has been said to be 90 percent of all human communication. Whether or not you agree with that percentage, you must admit that nonverbal messages are very frequent and powerful.

Cultures around the world have different customs about *touch*. Some want little or no public touch. Others will settle for the handshake. Others encourage lots of hugging, kissing, and back-slapping. The sexual component of public touch causes the most confusion. This chapter explains the cultural meanings of touch.

This chapter also opens up the strange and wonderful world of *gestures*. Gestures convey powerful meanings without words. Displayed here is a wide variety of gestures that can cause cross-cultural miscommunication.

A sign of friendship

A sign of affection

*Words in text set in bold type are listed aphabetically and defined in the Word Patterns section on pages 97–98 of this chapter.

Likewise, this chapter shows how *posture* (the way you hold your entire body) conveys cultural messages. Sitting erect, slouching, pointing your foot—all these have important meanings in different cultures. In addition, this chapter looks at *gaze* from many different angles. It examines direct eye contact, avoidance of eye contact, winking, staring, and other aspects of gaze.

Armed with the new knowledge you'll gain from this chapter, you can avoid many cross-cultural problems, confusions, and conflicts. Enter the world of touch, gesture, posture, and gaze. Let's get physical!

YOUR SUCCESS PATTERNS IN THIS CHAPTER

In this chapter you will use all four language skills and will develop the ability to:

- explain the importance of nonverbal communication;
- demonstrate cultural differences in touch;
- show different kinds of gestures and when they might be used;
- explain the cultural meanings of various postures;
- tell the significance of different kinds of gazes; and
- use many new learning strategies to make your studying easier.

Task 3.1 Evaluating

THINKING ABOUT YOURSELF

Step 1. Assess your current ability by circling the actions above that you can do *now.*

Step 2. Which actions did you *not* circle? These are the actions to which you can pay most attention in this chapter. (If you did not circle any of these actions, this chapter will go a long way toward helping you understand the physical aspects of culture.)

IT WORKS! Learning Strategy: Assessing Your Ability

CULTURAL PATTERN 1: TOUCH

Task 3.2 Prelistening

TALKING ABOUT TOUCH

Before you listen to the tape, discuss these questions with your friends: What kinds of touch are appropriate in which situations? Does this behavior differ from culture to culture?

Task 3.3 Listening

MAKING A CHART

IT WORKS! Learning Strategy: Making a Chart

While listening, create a chart about touching. On the left side, list the cultures that are mentioned. On the right side, write down information about what kinds of touch are okay in each culture. Here is an example of such a chart.

ACCEPTABLE TOUCH IN DIFFERENT CULTURES

CULTURES	TYPES OF ACCEPTABLE TOUCH
Middle East	Handholding with same sex
etc.	

Your tape has **"Please Touch (Sometimes)"** by Roger Axtell, from *Do's and Taboos Around the World,* 3rd ed. New York: John Wiley, 1993, pp. 43–44 [slightly adapted].

Task 3.4 Postlistening

CHECKING WITH OTHERS

Step 1. Share your chart (from the previous task) with others.
Step 2. Check to see if you have charted the same information. If not, replay the tape and verify what was said.
Step 3. Expand or correct your chart if needed.

CULTURE CLIP!

Touch may be twice as important to North Americans as to Japanese people, according to Dean Barnlund. The Japanese touch their children more in infancy and early childhood than North Americans touch their children. However, the situation changes at adolescence. Many Japanese teenagers have no physical contact at all with a parent or friend. Japanese adults restrict touch even more, along with facial movement and gestures.

A 1970s study reported by Michael Argyle considered the number of times couples (containing one female and one male) touched each other per hour in cafes in three cities: San Juan, Puerto Rico, Paris, and London. In San Juan, each couple averaged 180 touches per hour; in Paris, 110; and in London, none at all! As Genelle Morain (1987, p. 131) notes, "The London couples would be prime candidates for culture shock in an African culture where two people engaged in casual conversation intertwine their legs as they talk."

Task 3.5 Prereading

GREETING OTHERS

In a small group, demonstrate all the possible ways you can think of to greet another person. Is touching always part of a greeting?

Task 3.6 Reading

HIGHLIGHTING WITH AN UNDERLINE

IT WORKS! Learning Strategy: Highlighting

While reading, underline all the different kinds of touching you find in the story.

Should I touch or not?

Some cultures discourage touching in public among adults. These cultures have developed non-touching ways for people to greet each other. Two main ways are using the prayer position and bowing. In Cambodia, Sri Lanka, and Laos, the most common greeting is a non-touching prayer position. In this position, both hands are together at the chest level, and the higher the hands, the greater the respect. Bowing is another greeting that does not require touch. Many East Asians, such as Japanese, Koreans, Chinese, and Vietnamese, bow deeply to show humility and respect. Other non-touch greetings exist, too. People flick the eyebrows or nod the head (Fiji), pass a pipe or **snuff** (rural Mongolia), salute each other (Nepal), and kneel or clap (Zambia).

Sometimes rules exist against touch involving certain parts of the body in public. Of course, touching another person's sexual parts is typically off-limits in public. Touching a person's head, the most sacred part of the body, is forbidden in countries such as many Southeast Asian countries and in parts of the South Pacific. In many countries, the least sacred part of the body, the foot, is not allowed to touch anyone else.

In certain countries, people cannot touch certain other people. In Zambia, touching between parents-in-law and their children's spouses is not acceptable. In Buddhist countries, women cannot touch Buddhist monks.

Shaking Hands

In some cultures, shaking hands is the only form of public touch. For instance, in England, shaking hands lightly is fine, but other forms of touching (such as backslapping or putting an arm around the shoulder of a new **acquaintance**) are not common. People from such diverse cultures as the South Pacific, Eastern and Western Europe, and even the Far East and parts of Africa greet each other with a handshake and may wave at each other at a distance. In most of these countries other forms of touching in public are generally *not* encouraged. In other countries (in parts of Europe, Latin America, and the Middle East), handshaking can be followed (or substituted for) by an embrace or a kiss on the cheek.

In parts of Europe and other places, you can shake hands by offering your forearm, elbow, or shoulder to be shaken instead of your hand (especially if your hand is dirty). The handshake is light and quick in France, England, and certain other parts of the world influenced by these countries. It differs from the very firm, pumping, and continued U.S. handshake. The German handshake is firm but quite stiff.

In some places, handshakes are reserved for men. This happens frequently in parts of Africa, India, and the Middle East. In Korea, women and men use entirely different forms of handshakes! In countries where men and women are allowed to shake hands, the rules are complicated. In Eastern Europe, where women are allowed to shake hands, the woman must extend her hand before the man offers his, but in France and Russia, men must reach out first.

In Germany, a man shakes a woman's hand before he shakes the hand of another man. In some European countries—including Austria, Poland, and Romania—handshaking between women and men is sometimes accompanied by a kiss of the woman's hand by the man.

Physical Affection in Public

Many Middle Eastern and Asian countries discourage physical affection in public between unmarried males and females. However, kissing on both cheeks (or really brushing cheeks while kissing the air) is popular in countries around the world. Sometimes instead of a double kiss there is a triple kiss.

In many cultures, ranging from Africa and Latin America to the Middle East and the Far East, friends of same sex can hold hands when walking or speaking. They can also kiss and hug freely. In Israel, the United States, and in some Latin American countries, back-patting is common especially among male friends.

Source: Contains some concepts adapted from Culturgrams, Provo, Utah: Brigham Young University, 1992.

LEARNING STRATEGY

Managing Your Learning: Monitoring your understanding and your attention is very helpful.

Task 3.7 Postreading

MONITORING YOUR UNDERSTANDING AND ATTENTION

Step 1. Circle all the kinds of touch (or non-touch) that were mentioned above.

touching parents-in-law
bowing
using prayer-position greeting
kissing a person
eyebrow flicking
passing the pipe or snuff
touching someone with a foot
circling a hand above a head
saluting
shaking hands lightly
shaking hands with a limp wrist
nodding
kneeling
touching a person's head
touching spouses of one's children
kissing the air
clapping hands
touching the heart
covering the eyes
touching a Buddhist monk
shaking hands with pumping action
shaking hands stiffly
shaking wet hands
frowning

Task 3.8 Expanding Your Knowledge

COMPLETING THE HANDSHAKE CHART

Complete this chart to show the different kinds of handshakes and the countries where they are used. (Instead, you can create a different one of your own.)

HANDSHAKE CHART

KIND OF HANDSHAKE	COUNTRY OR COUNTRIES WHERE FOUND
Light, quick handshake	________________
Firm, stiff handshake	________________
Firm, pumping handshake	________________
Shaking elbows, forearms, or shoulders if hands are dirty	________________
Other handshakes:	
•	________________
•	________________

LEARNING STRATEGY

Personalizing: Expressing your preferences often helps you clarify your own cultural influences.

Task 3.9 Expanding Your Knowledge

TAKING THE PULSE

Step 1. Complete the opinion survey by circling YES or NO for each of the following items. (You might also want to put additional comments in the margin to explain.)

YOUR PREFERENCES ABOUT PUBLIC TOUCHING

Unmarried men and women can hold hands.	YES	NO
Married men and women can hold hands.	YES	NO
Two men can hold hands.	YES	NO
Two women can hold hands.	YES	NO
Children of the same sex can hold hands.	YES	NO
Unmarried men and women can kiss.	YES	NO
Married men and women can kiss.	YES	NO
Two men can kiss.	YES	NO
Two women can kiss.	YES	NO
Children of the same sex can kiss.	YES	NO
Unmarried men and women can hug.	YES	NO
Married men and women can hug.	YES	NO
Two men can hug.	YES	NO
Two women can hug.	YES	NO
Children of the same sex can hug.	YES	NO

Step 2. Compare your answers and any marginal comments with those of someone else, especially someone from a different culture from yours. What similarities do you find? What contrasts exist? Discuss any differences and explain the reasons to each other.

LEARNING STRATEGY

Forming Concepts: Separating fact (objective truth) from opinion or belief (subjective truth) is important in understanding other cultures.

Task 3.10 Expanding Your Knowledge

SEPARATING FACT FROM OPINION

Step 1. Which is a fact and which is an opinion? Put an X under FACT if the statement reflects objective or scientific reality, and put an X under OPINION if the statement reflects subjective or personal reality.

	Statement	FACT	OPINION
_____	**a.** In many parts of the world, men are not allowed to touch women in public.	_____	_____
_____	**b.** Women and men should not hug or kiss in public.	_____	_____
_____	**c.** It is best to be cautious about showing affection in public.	_____	_____
_____	**d.** A woman who allows a man to touch her in public must be a prostitute.	_____	_____
_____	**e.** It is a common occurrence in many countries that two men hug each other in public.	_____	_____
_____	**f.** Women are allowed to embrace and kiss in public in many cultures.	_____	_____
_____	**g.** Two people of the same sex who publicly hug or kiss are homosexuals.	_____	_____
_____	**h.** Public displays of affection are okay in many countries but not in others.	_____	_____
_____	**i.** In many cultures, children can usually touch each other in public more freely than adults.	_____	_____
_____	**j.** The amount and kind of touch that is acceptable should be decided by the individual, not by society.	_____	_____

Step 2. Now put a T to the left of the items you consider to be true. Put an F to the left of those you consider false.

Step 3. Discuss your findings with someone else. Do you agree about what is fact and what is opinion?

CULTURE CLIP!

In the United States, the principle of casualness sometimes competes with the rule of personal space. Even though people in the United States want a lot of personal space, they often touch strangers on the arm or the back. This kind of casual touching helps to break down the impersonal walls erected by the strong desire for personal space. Sometimes it shows a bid for friendship. In the same way, people from the United States casually use first names (almost immediately after meeting someone new). These signs of casualness should not *necessarily* be taken as signs of real friendship or closeness; the strong need still exists for personal space and private distance.

LEARNING STRATEGY

Managing Your Learning: Deciding to observe more closely increases your cultural awareness.

Task 3.11 Expanding Your Knowledge

EXPERIMENTING WITH GESTURES AND OBSERVING RESPONSES

Step 1. Try bowing, using prayer position, eyebrow flicking, kneeling, hand clapping, and the other kinds of non-touch greetings found early in this chapter.
Step 2. How do you and your friends feel about these?
Step 3. Are these greetings comfortable or uncomfortable?
Step 4. Why might they be perfect for some cultures but not for others?

Task 3.12 Expanding Your Knowledge

DOING A "TRUST FALL"

In certain Western cultures, groups are formed to teach people—often strangers or new acquaintances rather than close friends—to trust each other more effectively. One of the activities that such groups sometimes do is called a "trust fall."

Trust fall

Step 1. The group stands holding hands in a circle around one group member.

Step 2. That person stands in the center of the circle *with eyes closed* and then leans back, falling against the clasped hands of the people in the circle.

Step 3. The people in the circle support the falling person, thus creating a sense of trust.

Step 4. Soon they push the person toward another part of the circle.

Step 5. The person falls again against the hands and arms of people in the circle. This goes on for three to five minutes. The falling person always has people to lean on, and trust is supposed to grow—even if the people do not know each other.

Step 6. Discuss the reactions. How did it feel? Were there similar or different reactions from people from different cultures? Why did people respond the way they did?

Step 7. Discuss the reasons for the reactions. Which responses seemed culturally related? Is the acceptability of falling into another's arms the same in different cultures? Is the general concept of "trust" the same in different cultures? Explain.

Threads

The first step binds one to the second.

French proverb

Task 3.13 Expanding Your Knowledge

CREATING A CULTURAL GUIDEBOOK ON TOUCH

Create an illustrated cultural guidebook (5–10 pages) about touching in public, for the use of people who are new to the culture in which you currently find yourself. Or, if you want, make this guidebook bigger by adding suggestions about touching that would be applicable in different cultures.

Step 1. Be as specific as you can! The only useful rules about touch are the specific ones.

Step 2. Decorate the cover, include pictures, and make the list or guidebook look as interesting as possible.

Step 3. Share the guidebook with those who need it.

Step 4. Get feedback about its usefulness.

Step 5. Revise it if you think it is necessary to do so.

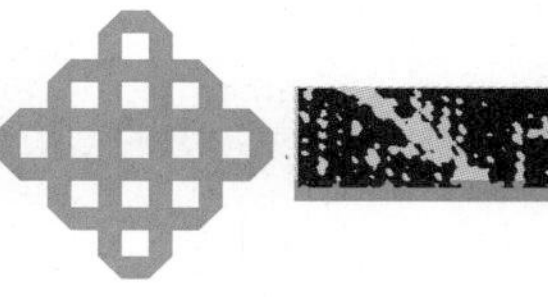

Task 3.14 Prelistening

THINKING ABOUT YOUR OWN MISTAKES

Discuss with others: Have you ever made a mistake in your use of gestures or body language? When, where, and what happened?

Storyteller using gestures

Task 3.15 Listening

FINDING THE MISTAKES

Listen for all the mistakes—or possible mistakes—suggested on the tape in "Risky Body Language." Find at least four. Write them down as you listen.

Your tape has **"Risky Body Language,"** by Roger Axtell, from *Do's and Taboos Around the World,* 3rd ed. New York: John Wiley, pp. 41, 43.

Task 3.16 Postlistening

REVIEWING THE MEANING OF CERTAIN GESTURES

Step 1. What does the circled thumb and forefinger mean to North Americans?
Step 2. What does it mean to people from most other parts of the world?
Step 3. What can go wrong when you give an innocent wink or nod?
Step 4. What are two different interpretations of the ordinary American wave?
Step 5. Demonstrate the American wave and the European wave.
Step 6. Why would you avoid the thumb-out hitchhiking sign?

Task 3.17 Prereading

PREDICTING

IT WORKS! Learning Strategy: Predicting

Step 1. Do you predict that there are any universal gestures? If so, what might some of those gestures be?

Step 2. Do you predict there are gestures that are special to certain cultures? If so, what might some of those gestures be?

Task 3.18 Reading

Threads

Come on baby, let's do the twist!

Chubby Checker

CONTRASTING THE UNIVERSAL AND THE SPECIFIC

As you read, try to find and remember the gestures that are universal. Contrast those with any gestures that might be specific to a given culture.

Universal and culture-specific gestures

Many small but important facts are contained in the nonver-bal world of gestures. Let's first consider the most universal gestures of all and then discuss the ones that differ widely around the globe.

Universal Gestures

Here are some very common gestures used in many cultures and probably understandable in almost all cultures. Rubbing or patting your stomach usually means you have had enough to eat. Putting your head in a sleeping-type position conveys the idea that you want to sleep. Other gestures regarding bodily functions are often understood across cultures.

A gesture that **anthropologists** call the "eyebrow flash" (a raise of the eyebrow for one-sixth of a second, then a lowering) appears in numerous cultures throughout Europe, the South Pacific, and South America. It means the person is ready for social contact and is usually used during a greeting.

Certain angry facial expressions (which are not really gestures but are strongly related to them) have occurred in many cultures and are found even in the deaf-blind, who did not learn by imitating others. Other primary emotions, such as happiness, sadness, fear, surprise, and disgust, have corresponding facial expressions that appear in people in Borneo, Brazil, Japan, and the United States. Each culture has its own rules about *when* to display these emotions.

Culture-Specific Gestures

However, many other gestures have meanings that are often completely mis-understood by people in other cultures. For example, former doctoral student Lois Bursack filmed men and women in Minneapolis, a major city in the United States These men and women were intentionally trying to make gestures that expressed "agreement" and "courtesy" without the use of words. The film sequences were studied by adults in Beirut, Lebanon; Tokyo, Japan; and Bogota, Colombia. The viewers were unable to figure out what the U.S. people's gestures meant.

Source: Contains some concepts adapted from Genelle Morain, "Kinesics and Cross-Cultural Understanding," in Louise F. Luce and Elise C. Smith (eds.), Toward Internationalism: Readings in Cross-Cultural Communication. Cambridge, Mass.: Newbury House / Harper & Row, pp. 117–142.

LEARNING STRATEGY

Forming Concepts: Separating aspects that happen everywhere (universal) and those that happen in only certain cultures (culture-specific) helps you better understand culture.

Some universally understood gestures showing "I'm hungry," "I'm tired," and "I'm ready to talk.

Task 3.19 Postreading

CONSIDERING THE MOTIVATION FOR USING GESTURES

Step 1. According to the story, what kind of gestures seem to occur everywhere? Why?

Step 2. We are all human beings. So why are not *all* gestures universal? Why do some cultures have their own particular gestures? What motivations are behind these gestures?

Step 3. Discuss your findings with a small group.

IT WORKS! Learning Strategy: Delving into Motivations

CULTURE CLIP!

Gesture-loving cultures include Israel, France, Italy, Portugal, Mexico, Costa Rica, Guatemala, Bolivia, Jamaica, and many African and Middle Eastern countries. However, the U.S. mainstream culture uses hand and arm gestures only moderately—but it makes up for the lack of such gestures by having very animated facial expressions (including smiling at total strangers). Other U.S. cultures or subcultures that are influenced by Africa and Latin America use hand and arm gestures much more than the U.S. mainstream culture. Certain cultures do not use many hand and arm gestures and consider them impolite. Surprisingly, some of these cultures are in Latin America: for example, El Salvador and Chile. Not so surprisingly, many Northern European countries dislike frequent gesturing.

Task 3.20 Prelistening

COMPARING GESTURES

What is the most common gesture for showing approval or happiness in your culture? For showing disapproval? Compare with people from other cultures.

LEARNING STRATEGY

Remembering New Material: Physically acting out new information helps you to remember it.

Task 3.21 Listening

ACTING IT OUT

While listening, act out each gesture (except for the ones you find to be obscene in your culture). Make sure you know what each gesture is. Refer to the pictures if you don't know a gesture.

Your tape has **"Gestures of Approval and Disapproval."**

Gestures of Approval

Thumbs-up in France

Two-thumbs-up in Kenya

Fingers together in a hand purse in Tunisia

Tilted head in Greece

Downward nod in Lebanon

Raised eyebrows in Tonga

Cheek screw in Italy

Fingertip kiss in Europe and Latin America

The shaking hand in Latin America and the Far East

Puckering lips in Barbados

Thumbs-up in Bangladesh

Upward nod in Greece

The fig in Europe

The chin flick in Italy

Gestures Showing Disapproval

LEARNING STRATEGY

Remembering New Material: Using a standard outline form can help you remember what you read.

Task 3.22 Postlistening

OUTLINING

Step 1. Probably you know the standard outline form. Start with the Roman numerals I, II, and III to indicate the most important points in the listening passage. These are:

I. THE "O" OR OK SIGN
II. GESTURES OF APPROVAL OR "YES"
III. GESTURES OF DISAPPROVAL OR "NO"

Write these main points down on a separate sheet using Roman numerals.

Step 2. Beneath each of the main points, use the letters A, B, C, and so on to indicate the points that have the next greatest importance. For instance, under Roman numeral I you might list:

A. OK sign is fine in the United States
B. OK sign is vulgar in Brazil.
C. OK sign is rude in Russia . . . .
. . . OK sign means "worthless" in France.

For Roman numerals II and III, list all the secondary points with A, B, and C.

Step 3. If there are any points of least importance that would fall under the letters (A, B, C, and so on), signify these with Arabic numbers—1, 2, and so on.

Step 4. Reread the passage. Is there anything you want to change about the outline? If so, go ahead.

Step 5. Now review the outline several times to help you remember what you read.

Task 3.23 Prereading

LOOKING AT THE MAP

Before you read, look at the map or globe and find the following places mentioned in the reading: Argentina, Bangladesh, Barbados, Brazil, Ecuador, El Salvador, Egypt, Fiji, Finland, Germany, Guinea-Bissau, Indonesia, Kenya, Malaysia, Mexico, Mongolia, Netherlands, Pakistan, Peru, Portugal, Republic of Ireland, Russia, Taiwan, Tonga, Switzerland, United States, Wales.

Task 3.24 Reading

PERSONALIZING

As you read, consider whether you have seen any of these gestures before, and if so, when and where. Have you used any of these yourself?

More hand gestures

Beckoning and Waving

In the United States, the "come here" **(beckoning)** gesture involves waving all fingers, or sometimes just the index finger, with the palm up. But in many cultures, waving the fingers (especially the index finger) with the palm up is vulgar. People in many Asian, Middle Eastern, and Latin cultures beckon by waving all the fingers of one hand with the palm down. In Kenya, all fingers should be waved, with the palm facing either down or up. In Portugal, all fingers must be waved with the palm up. For people on the island of Tonga, a downward wave of the arm is beckoning. So watch out how you wave!

Sometimes you are not allowed to beckon certain people with gestures. In Malaysia, Tonga, Bangladesh, and Indonesia, for instance, you can beckon only children and a few service workers using hand gestures. Chileans beckon only waiters with hand gestures. In El Salvador, only close friends are beckoned by a wave of the arm.

Mexico and Brazil do not beckon by hand but instead use the "psst-psst" sound. In other cultures, including the United States, a person sometimes whistles to call someone (though whistling is more often used to call a pet dog!). But never whistle to get someone's attention in Ecuador and Brazil!

Pointing It Out

People in the United States and some European countries point by extending the index finger. Most other cultures believe that pointing with index finger should not be allowed at all and that you must use whole hand to point. Pointing at people is rude in many countries.

Some cultures, such as Pakistan, Malaysia, and the Republic of Ireland (Eire), discourage the use of finger gestures for any purpose, not just for pointing. These cultures consider it rude to use fingers for gesturing. Pointing with the lips is done by Native Americans,

Mongolians, and some Africans and Latins. People in Bangladesh and India point with their chins. In Guinea-Bissau, pointing is done with the tongue.

Some cultures encourage pointing at one's head or one's body. For instance, in Taiwan people referring to themselves in conversation should point at their noses. In the United States, people frequently point a finger toward themselves to emphasize how they feel or think. Also in the United States, pointing the index finger at your own head or circling that finger around the ear suggests that another person (who is the subject of your conversation) is crazy. This very gesture is a serious insult in Switzerland, the Netherlands, and Germany. On the other hand, in the Netherlands, the circling finger by the ear can also mean someone has a telephone call. In Peru and Argentina, the finger pointing to the head has nothing to do with craziness or telephones; it can mean "I am thinking" or "You should think."

Showing Height

Showing the height of a person, animal, or object can be quite a task if you don't know the right gesture to use. In the United States, people tend to use an outstretched arm to show the heights of all three. But in Egypt, the outstretched arm is only used to show an animal's height. In Mexico, one can show the height of a person by vertically extending the arm with the index finger out and the rest of the fingers folded. The height of an animal is indicated by the outstretched arm, with the thumb up. The height of an inanimate object is shown by the outstretched arm with the palm down.

Folded Arms

For people in Barbados, folded arms mean paying complete attention. In the United States, folded arms often mean impatience or anger. In Russia, talking with arms folded across the chest is rude, but in Wales it is perfectly okay to do so. Folded arms in Finland signify **arrogance** and pride, while in Fiji this gesture means disrespect. Placing hands on hips is disrespectful or **defiant** in Argentina, Barbados, and sometimes in the United States. At other times in the United States, this gesture simply means "I'm waiting impatiently."

Task 3.25 Postreading

MAKING A PERSONALIZED CHART

IT WORKS! Learning Strategy: Linking with Your Own Experience

Using the reading passage above, list the key gestures, the cultures where they are found, and the meanings. Also indicate where and when you saw any of the gestures personally.

YOUR PERSONALIZED CHART OF IMPORTANT GESTURES

GESTURE	CULTURE	MEANING	WHERE/WHEN I SAW THIS GESTURE
1.			
2.			
3.			
4.			
5.			
6.			
and so on . . .			

Task 3.26 Prelistening

ASKING ABOUT IMPRESSIONS

Discuss with others: What is the impression you get when you see someone spit, scratch, use a toothpick, throw objects, talk with hands in pockets, make horns over someone else's head, pull down the eyeskin, or rub thumbs together? If you don't know the meanings of all these gestures, don't worry—you'll soon find out!

Task 3.27 Listening

DISTINGUISHING BETWEEN USEFUL AND DANGEROUS GESTURES

As you listen, consider which of the gestures you would like to use; on a separate sheet, give each of these gestures a plus (+). Think of which of the gestures might get you in trouble, and give each of them a minus (-).

Your tape has **"Other Gestures,"** which contains some concepts adapted from *Culturgrams*, Provo, Utah: Brigham Young University, 1992.

LEARNING STRATEGY

Forming Concepts: Role-playing helps you understand cultural concepts quickly and enjoyably.

Task 3.28 Postlistening

ROLE-PLAYING THE GESTURES

With a group of five to eight people (if possible from different cultures), create a role-play including as many of the gestures above as you can. To do this:

Step 1. Develop a story with characters. Make role-cards for them so they know what their roles are and which cultures they represent.
Step 2. Have them travel to different countries and see (or use) different gestures.
Step 3. Be sure to make the responses culturally authentic—positive when a gesture is used correctly in a culture, negative when a gesture is used incorrectly in a culture.
Step 4. Discuss the role-play afterwards. Find out what was comfortable and what was not. Check on the appropriate use of gestures in different cultures during the role-play.

Task 3.29 Expanding Your Knowledge

WATCHING FOREIGN FILMS

Step 1. Make a point to watch two or three foreign films soon. When you watch them, notice all the gestures.
Step 2. While watching such films, consider these questions: Are any of them familiar to you from this chapter? Do you see any that show scorn, rejection, happiness, approval, beckoning, pointing, obscenity?
Step 3. Discuss with others: What can you learn about cultures and people from watching gestures in foreign films? What can you learn about yourself?

Task 3.30 Expanding Your Knowledge

EXAMINING YOUR OWN GESTURES

Step 1. We often forget to look at our own gestures. In front of a mirror, do the following:
- **a.** Gesture as though you are happy with something or someone.
- **b.** Gesture "Go away!" or "That's terrible!" Gesture "Come here."
- **c.** Gesture showing the height of a person and the height of an animal. (Are these height gestures different or the same?)
- **d.** Gesture "I'm tired of waiting for you."
- **e.** Act out any other gestures you want.

Step 2. Are your forms of these gestures similar to any mentioned in this chapter? Explain.

Task 3.31 Expanding Your Knowledge

NOTICING THE GESTURES OF PEOPLE AROUND YOU

Step 1. During one day, take a tiny notebook and jot down all the gestures you see people making and what you think each gesture means.
Step 2. Then at the end of the day organize the list by the types of gestures.
Step 3. Consider whether any of the gestures are different from those you might have used.
Step 4. Jot down any cultural influences that might cause any such differences.
Step 5. Discuss the gestures on your list with at least one other person.

Task 3.32 Expanding Your Knowledge

CONSIDERING THE MOST OFFENSIVE GESTURES

Step 1. In your culture, what are the most offensive gestures, and why?
Step 2. Are they mainly sexual, or do they have other meanings?
Step 3. Are these gestures also rude in other cultures?
Step 4. Discuss these gestures with a friend who is from another culture.

Task 3.33 Expanding Your Knowledge

TRYING TO AVOID MISTAKES

Discuss with another person:

1. How can you avoid making big cultural mistakes with gestures?
2. Besides this chapter, what other resources do you have to help you know about gestures?
3. When is a gesture-related mistake serious, and when is it unimportant?

CULTURAL PATTERN 3: POSTURE

Task 3.34 Prereading

THINKING ABOUT POSTURE

With a group of friends, slouch over and put your feet on the table. Get reactions from your friends as to the impression this posture gives. Does it signify friendliness, casualness, disrespect, or something else?

Task 3.35 Reading

CONSIDERING THE IMPORTANCE OF POSTURE

As you read, consider the importance of posture, especially at the time you first meet someone. Think about all the different postures mentioned here. Take notes or underline the most important points if you wish.

Posture talks

Posture means how a person sits or stands. Sometimes posture is called "bearing" because it involves how a person bears (carries) herself or himself. Around the globe, posture means different things in different cultures.

In the United States, where "casualness" is considered a great virtue, people often sit with feet on chairs or even desks. They sometimes sit with their backsides (buttocks) on tables and desks as a way of expressing their individuality or carefree attitude. They feel comfortable crossing their legs and sitting with one ankle on the other knee. Poor posture—**slumping** oneself over while sitting in a chair and while placing feet on whatever object is around —is a common U.S. behavior. It is designed to show that the person is casual, honest, sincere, and "just one of the folks." In the United States, even millionaires, corporation presidents, government leaders, and movie stars try to pretend they are ordinary people by using "the U.S. **slouch**" and "the feet-on-the-furniture" maneuver.

Unfortunately, other countries interpret this behavior as being sloppy and as reflecting a general lack of alertness, interest, and respect. People from the United States do not usually realize that what they think of as casualness is viewed very differently and very negatively by many people around the world.

People in many cultures are expected to sit erect. Such cultures include many countries in Latin America, Asia, Europe, and the Middle East. In the United States, slouching is acceptable and is a positive sign of being casual and friendly.

In the United States, crossing legs is a sign of *good* etiquette. Many cultures say that crossing legs is okay, but placing the ankle on the knee while crossing one's legs is totally unacceptable. You can cross your legs but not put your ankle on your knee in some Latin and Asian countries. In Peru, men can place the ankle on knee, but women must cross their entire legs at the knee. In Syria women must not cross their legs at all in public, though men can cross at the knee. In Hong Kong, women are allowed to cross their legs except among the traditional Chinese.

One reason for not putting the ankle on the knee is that when you do so, one foot or the sole of the shoe is usually pointing at someone. This is a very severe insult in many countries around the world, *especially Muslim countries.* Under few circumstances should you point your foot at anyone, because the foot is considered the least sacred part of the body in many societies. In some countries such as Nepal, pointing the foot at a cow is an outrage, because the cow is a sacred animal. In Buddhist countries, pointing the foot at statue of the Buddha is a severe offense. Moving objects with the feet is very rude in Thailand, Nepal, and Taiwan. In Bangladesh, you should not touch books with a foot or shoe; if you do, you must make an elaborate apology. In some countries it is prohibited to cross one's legs at all (usually for fear that the sole of the foot will show or point toward someone). These countries include Morocco, Nigeria, Thailand, and most of the Islamic or Muslim countries. In Turkey and Mongolia, you must not cross your legs in front of a superior or elder.

As you can tell, posture is a very strong messenger. It conveys much about a particular person. Posture (in many cultures) says something about the person's honesty, alertness, intelligence, religiousness, respect, and overall decency—or the *opposite* of all of these! Posture tells people whether they want to get to know a stranger, and it also tells what to think about the people they already know.

The problem with your trying to "read" someone else's posture is that your culture may interpret posture differently from that person's culture. Cultural confusions are frequent regarding body posture. Prevent trouble by remembering some key facts about posture in different cultures!

Task 3.36 Postreading

SURVEYING THE POSTURES

Step 1. Circle any of the following postures you think are *acceptable in most cultures.*

arms over back of a chair
slouching in a chair
sitting with a straight back
crossing legs at the knees
uncrossed legs
ankle on the knee
pointing the foot
showing the sole of the foot
moving objects with the feet
touching objects with the feet
keeping the feet on the floor
feet on a table

Threads

There's language in her eye, her cheek, her lip, Nay, her foot speaks.

William Shakespeare

Step 2. In the list above, put a check beside any postures that would be *unacceptable in most cultures.*
Step 3. Why is it important to know the difference between acceptable and unacceptable postures?
Step 4. Discuss your findings with others.

Task 3.37 Prelistening

EMPATHIZING

IT WORKS! Learning Strategy: Empathizing with Someone

Imagine you are a business executive, like Bob, on your first trip to the Far East. What aspects of posture would you want to know about?

Task 3.38 Listening

THINKING ABOUT BOB AND HIS HOSTS

As you listen, think about how Bob feels when he keeps making mistakes. Think about how his hosts feel when he makes mistakes.

Your tape has **"I Slouched My Way to a Cross-Cultural Insult,"** by Bob Tripp. Used with permission.

Bob makes cross-cultural mistakes with his posture.

Task 3.39 Postlistening

LISTING ALL THE MISTAKES

Step 1. In your notebook list all the mistakes that Bob made in Japan.
Step 2. How do the Japanese interpret his behavior?
Step 3. Are the Japanese likely to explain their attitudes about his behavior to Bob himself? Why or why not?
Step 4. What would help Bob?
Step 5. Discuss your responses with someone else. Note any cultural differences.

Task 3.40 Expanding Your Knowledge

SEARCHING FOR DIFFERENT POSTURES

Step 1. Go to a movie and look at the postures of the actors and actresses. Or leaf through family photos to see the postures of your family members. Or take a good look at people in your class or in a business meeting. Take notes if possible.

Step 2. What kinds of postures do you see? Are people erect or slumped? Are they sitting with feet on the floor or in any number of cross-legged poses?

Step 3. What do these postures tell you? What would these postures tell someone from the Middle East? From Japan or Korea? From the United States? From Britain?

Task 3.41 Expanding Your Knowledge

MAKING A POSTURE VIDEO

Step 1. Make a video of people from different cultures (or from one culture) standing and sitting in their normal postures.

Step 2. Discuss: What do these postures convey or express? How might people from other cultures interpret these postures differently from the way they were intended?

LEARNING STRATEGY

Managing Your Learning: Evaluating your own behaviors can help you develop better cross-cultural skills.

Task 3.42 Expanding Your Knowledge

ASSESSING YOUR PERSONAL BEHAVIORS

Step 1. Based on this chapter so far, do you ever do anything (regarding gesture or posture) that might be offensive to someone in another culture?

Step 2. If the answer is yes, which it would be for most people, list the things you do that might cause problems to people in another culture.

Step 3. How can you be sensitive to these behaviors?

Step 4. Should you try to avoid these behaviors when you are around people from another culture that might not like them? Or should the other people adapt themselves to you? Under what circumstances should someone change? Explain.

Step 5. Discuss your ideas with someone else. See if your ideas change as a result of this discussion.

Task 3.43 Prereading

PRACTICING EYE MOVEMENTS

With other people, practice eye movements, including: looking out the corner of your eye, gazing under **dropped** lids, eyes wide open in a startled expression, rolling your eyes, looking down when someone passes, and so on. See how each movement feels to you and the impression it gives to others.

Threads

Drink to me only with thine eyes.

Poet Ben Jonson

Task 3.44 Reading

LEARNING EYE LANGUAGE

As you read this short passage, think of the eyes as having a language of their own. List as many meanings as you find here in that eye language.

Eye language

by Roger Axtell

Just back from a tour of several Arabian Gulf countries, a woman recalls how jumpy she felt talking to men there. "Not because of what they said," she explains, "but what they did with their eyes." Instead of the occasional blink, Arabs lower their lids so slowly and languorously that she was convinced they were falling asleep.

In Japan eye contact is a key to the way you feel about someone. And the less of it, the better. What a Westerner considers an honest look in the eye, the Oriental takes as a lack of respect and a personal affront. Even when shaking hands or bowing—and especially when conversing—only an occasional glance into the other person's face is considered polite. The rest of the time, great attention should be paid to fingertips, desk tops, and the warp and woof of the carpet.

"Always keep your shoes shined in Tokyo," advises an electronics representative who has logged many hours there. "You can bet a lot of Japanese you meet will have their eyes on them."

Source: Roger Axtell, Do's and Taboos Around the World, 3rd ed. New York: John Wiley, p. 42.

Task 3.45 Postreading

CHECKING YOUR LEARNING OF EYE LANGUAGE

Step 1. According to the reading, which culture dislikes direct eye contact?
Step 2. Which culture likes direct eye contact?
Step 3. Why was the woman visitor nervous in the Middle East?

Task 3.46 Prelistening

KEEP BUILDING YOUR EYE LANGUAGE

Practice the following in a small group: Staring strongly, winking, looking away, looking steadily, looking at the floor. What meanings do each of these eye movements convey?

Threads

The eyes are the window of the soul.

Common international saying

Task 3.47 Listening

CATCHING THE INFORMATION WHILE YOU LISTEN

Using this chart, take notes while listening. (Add more lines if you desire.)

IT WORKS! Learning Strategy: Making a Chart

CHART OF ACCEPTABLE GAZING

NAME OF CULTURE		
____________	________	should not look directly into the eyes of ________
____________	________	should not look directly into the eyes of ________
____________	________	should not look directly into the eyes of ________
____________	________	should not look directly into the eyes of ________
____________	________	should not look directly into the eyes of ________
____________	________	should not look directly into the eyes of ________
____________	________	may look directly into the eyes of ________
____________	________	may look directly into the eyes of ________
____________	________	may look directly into the eyes of ________
____________	________	may look directly into the eyes of ________
____________	________	may wink at ________
____________	________	may stare at ________

Your tape has **"Here's Looking at You!"**

Task 3.48 Postlistening

GIVING REASONS

Step 1. What are some reasons that certain cultures do not believe people should use direct eye contact? (You might have to infer or guess reasons.)

Step 2. Why is direct eye contact permitted in other cultures? (Again, infer or guess if you don't know for sure.)

Task 3.49 Prereading

THINKING ABOUT RESPECT

Discuss with others: What messages are given when a person looks down at the floor? How does this differ across cultures?

Task 3.50 Reading

FINDING THE TRUTH

Step 1. Indicate the things that are true and those that are false about Livia as you read. Put an "X" under TRUE if a phrase is true or under FALSE if it is false. If a statement is neither mentioned nor implied, put an "X" in that column.

Livia . . .	**TRUE**	**FALSE**	**NOT MENTIONED OR IMPLIED**
is a high school student	_____	_____	_____
is Cuban	_____	_____	_____
is a teenager	_____	_____	_____
has two brothers	_____	_____	_____
is female	_____	_____	_____
is 15 years old	_____	_____	_____
doesn't respect authority	_____	_____	_____
likes to study	_____	_____	_____
is a troublemaker	_____	_____	_____
smokes a lot	_____	_____	_____
is sly or devious	_____	_____	_____
likes her school	_____	_____	_____
is misunderstood because of her culture	_____	_____	_____
lives in New York	_____	_____	_____
has dark hair	_____	_____	_____

The story of Livia

by Julius Fast

The significance of looking is universal, but usually we are not sure of just how we look or how we are looked at. Honesty demands, in our culture, that we look someone straight in the eye [but not for too long]. Other cultures have other rules, as a principal in a New York City high school recently discovered.

A young girl at the high school, a fifteen-year-old Puerto Rican, had been caught in the washroom with a group of girls suspected of smoking. Most of the group were known troublemakers, and while this young girl, Livia, had no record, the principal after a brief interview was convinced of her guilt and decided to suspend her with the others.

"It wasn't what she said," he reported later. "It was simply her attitude. There was something sly and suspicious about her. She just wouldn't meet my eye. She wouldn't look at me."

It was true. Livia at her interview with the principal stared down at the floor in what was a clear-cut guilty attitude and refused to meet his eyes.

"But she's a good girl," Livia's mother insisted. Not to the school, for she was too much of a "troublemaker" the principal felt, to come to the authorities with her protest. Instead, she turned to her neighbors and friends. As a result there was a demonstration of Puerto Rican parents at the school the next morning and the ugly **stirrings** of a threatened riot.

Fortunately, John Flores taught Spanish literature at the school, and John lived only a few doors from Livia and her family. Summoning his own courage, John asked for an interview with the principal.

"I know Livia and her parents," he told the principal. "And she's a good girl. I am sure there has been some mistake in this whole matter."

"If there was a mistake," the principal said uneasily, "I'll be glad to rectify it. There are thirty mothers outside yelling for my blood. But I questioned the child myself, and if I ever saw guilt written on a face—she wouldn't even meet my eyes!"

John drew a sign of relief, and then very carefully, for he was too new in the school to want to tread on toes, he explained some basic facts of Puerto Rican culture to the principal.

"In Puerto Rico a nice girl, a good girl," he explained, "does not meet the eyes of an adult. Refusing to do so is a sign of respect and obedience. It would be as difficult for Livia to look you in the eyes as it would be for her to misbehave, or for her mother to come to you with a complaint. In our culture, this is just not accepted behavior for a respectable family."

Fortunately the principal was a man who knew how to admit that he was wrong. He called Livia and her parents and the most vocal neighbors in and once again discussed the problem. In the light of John Flores's explanation it became obvious to him that Livia was not avoiding his eyes out of defiance, but out of a basic **demureness.** Her slyness, he now saw, was shyness. In fact, as the conference progressed and the parents relaxed, he realized that Livia was indeed a gentle and sweet girl.

Task 3.51 Postreading

GIVING OPINIONS

Write your opinions in the spaces provided, then discuss them with someone else.

Step 1. How could the principal have so clearly misinterpreted Livia's behavior?
Step 2. Why did the mother talk to the neighbors rather than going directly to the principal?
Step 3. What was John Flores's role in resolving the problem?
Step 4. This story ended positively, thanks to John Flores. What happens in situations where there is no one like John to **intervene**?
Step 5. Are you comfortable when a child looks an adult directly in the eye? Explain.
Step 6. Discuss your findings with somebody else. See if you can find someone who comes from a culture where looking down is a sign of respect for authority. Do you share the same perspectives on Livia's story?

Task 3.52 Prelistening

MOTHERING

Discuss: Consider what it might be like to have a mother from a traditional culture and to be a daughter or son living in a modern culture. What conflicts might occur?

Task 3.53 Listening

SEARCHING FOR THE EYES

IT WORKS! Learning Strategy: Delving into Motivations

While listening, pay attention to where the people in the story direct their gaze. Do they look at each other, at the floor, or elsewhere? Why might they do this?

Your tape has **"Double Face"** by Amy Tan, excerpted from *The Joy Luck Club,* New York: G. P. Putnam's Sons, 1989, pp. 254–256.

Novelist Amy Tan

Task 3.54 Postlistening

GAZING

Step 1. Reread these words of the mother, "Americans don't really look at one another when talking. They talk at their reflections. They look at others or themselves only when they think nobody is watching." Is this statement true or false? Explain.
Step 2. What is the conflict between the daughter and the mother?
Step 3. What does the mother see in the mirror toward the end of the story?
Step 4. What does that image mean to the mother?
Step 5. What do you think the daughter is thinking at the end?
Step 6. Discuss your findings with someone else and compare.

Task 3.55 Expanding Your Knowledge

MAKING A CONCEPT MAP OF GAZING

IT WORKS! Learning Strategy: Making a Concept Map

Step 1. Consider all you have read about gaze. Review the last part of this chapter (about gaze).

Step 2. Make a concept map of gaze. If you need to review how to do this, go back to Chapter 2. Be sure to include the different attitudes and beliefs about gaze in different cultures (encouragement of direct eye contact, avoidance of direct eye contact, winking as a sexual sign, winking to the children, and so forth).

Step 3. If you want, you can include the names of specific cultures or countries in your concept map.

Step 4. Compare your map with that of someone else. What differences and similarities are there? Are there any differences that are related to culture?

Task 3.56 Expanding Your Knowledge

LOOKING THROUGH MAGAZINES FOR GAZES

Step 1. Look through five or six picture-type magazines. Count the number of pictures in which

- people are looking directly at each other,
- people are avoiding eye contact with each other,
- people are winking at each other (note the meanings), and
- people are staring at each other (note the meanings).

Step 2. Discuss: Would you find the same results in other cultures? Why or why not?

Task 3.57 Expanding Your Knowledge

CONSIDERING YOUR IMPRESSIONS

For each of the following descriptions, indicate whether you think you would LIKE or DISLIKE the person. Put an "X" in the appropriate column.

A person who . . .	**LIKE**	**DISLIKE**
winks at you in a sexy way	________	________
winks at you in a "we-have-a-secret" way	________	________
stares at your face	________	________
stares at your body	________	________
stares at the ring on your finger	________	________
looks you straight in the eye	________	________
looks at the floor	________	________
looks behind you	________	________
looks at your neck	________	________
sits up straight	________	________
slumps in the chair	________	________
puts feet on the footstool	________	________
puts feet on *his or her* table	________	________
puts feet on *your* table	________	________
points a foot at you	________	________
points a foot at your child	________	________
points a foot at a religious statue	________	________

Add other actions in your notebook.

Threads

parts of me are pinned to earth, parts of me undermine song, parts of me spread on the water

Poet Wendy Rose

Task 3.58 Expanding Your Knowledge

CREATING A TWO-PAGE "TIP SHEET" ABOUT TOUCH, GESTURE, GAZE, AND POSTURE

Help newcomers to this culture by creating and publishing a factual two-page "tip sheet" (front and back of one sheet for easy use) containing suggestions about touch, gesture, gaze, and posture. Include only the things that newcomers *absolutely need to know.*

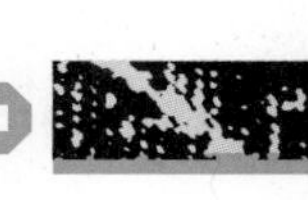

LEARNING STRATEGY

Remembering New Material: Drawing quick, simple pictures to go with words helps you remember the words effectively.

Task 3.59 Wordbuilding

DRAWING PICTURES TO LEARN VOCABULARY

Step 1. Many of the words below, which have been marked throughout this chapter, are related to the body. Therefore, it is easy to draw pictures of them to help you remember them. Pick out all the words that are "physical" (such as frowning, kowtowing, puckering, gazes, beckoning—these are just a few of the many!). Make simple, rapid line drawings of these words, and write each word next to the correct drawing.

Step 2. Optional: For fun, separate the words from the drawings and try to match them up!

Step 3. For the nonphysical words (of which there are few), make flashcards.

acquaintance—a person whom one knows only slightly
anthropologists—specialists in the science that studies human beings and their social behavior
arrogance—haughtiness, an overbearing manner
assertive—dominating, allowing no denial or opposition
averting—turning away or aside
beckoning—summoning, calling someone toward oneself with a gesture
clinched—settled, made conclusive (as in the deal is clinched)
defiant—showing a deliberate challenge (to authority) by disobedience
demureness—modesty, quietness
dropped—lowered, hung down
exotic—foreign, strange
folksy—very sociable (especially of people in or from small communities)
frowning—having a wrinkled brow, as in displeasure, puzzlement, or deep thought
gazes—looks (often long, intent looks)
hitchhiking—traveling by begging free rides in motor vehicles
inhabitants—permanent residents in a place
insult—a remark or act showing contempt and calculated to offend someone
intervene—to happen or cut in between points of time
jerking up—moving by applying a short, sudden force
kinky—of peculiar tastes in sexual satisfaction, now typically means unusual or odd

kowtowing—kneeling, touching the ground with the forehead, as a token of homage or deep respect among the Chinese; now means to humble oneself in a servile way
mullah's—belonging to a Muslim teacher of theology and sacred law
obsequious—so self-abasing as to lack a proper degree of personal dignity
outbow—to bow lower than the other person
puckering—gathering into narrow folds or wrinkles
punctuate—to interrupt by, or intersperse with, sound or gesture
repentance—a feeling of contrition or act of penance for sins committed
slouch—a bad posture or manner of walking, with drooping back and shoulders and loose, lax muscles and limbs
slumping—assuming a drooping posture
snuff—powdered tobacco inhaled into the nose
stirrings—strong emotions (can be of an idealistic kind)
vulgar—indecent, offensive

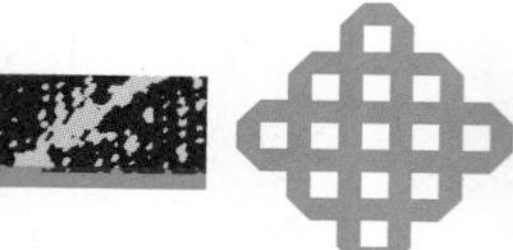

CHECKING YOUR SUCCESS

Task 3.60 Evaluating

REVIEWING THE OBJECTIVES AND RATING YOURSELF

IT WORKS! Learning Strategy: Assessing Your Ability

Circle YES or NO below.

Can you . . .

- explain the importance of nonverbal communication? YES NO
- demonstrate cultural differences in touch? YES NO
- show different kinds of gestures and when they might be used? YES NO
- explain the cultural meanings of various postures? YES NO
- tell the significance of different kinds of gazes? YES NO
- use many new learning strategies to make your studying easier? YES NO

WHERE TO GO FOR MORE INFORMATION

Argyle, Michael (1975). *Bodily communication.* New York: International Universities Press.

Argyle, Michael, and Mark Cook (1976). *Gaze and mutual gaze.* Cambridge: Cambridge University Press.

Axtell, Roger (ed.) (1993). *Do's and taboos around the world,* 3rd ed. New York: John Wiley.

Barnlund, Dean C. (1975). *Public and private self in Japan and the United States.* Tokyo: Simul Press.

Bursack, Lois (1970). *North American nonverbal behavior as perceived in three overseas urban cultures.* Ph.D. Dissertation, University of Minnesota.

David M. Kennedy Center (1992). *Culturgrams.* Provo, Utah: Brigham Young University.

Davis, Flora (1975). *Inside intuition.* New York: Signet.

Eibl-Eibesfeldt, I. (1974). Similarities and differences between cultures in expressive movements. In Shirley Weitz (ed.), *Nonverbal communication: Readings with commentary* (pp. 22–27). New York: Oxford University Press.

Ekman, Paul, Wallace V. Friesen, & Phoebe Ellsworth (1972). *Emotions in the human face.* New York: Pergamon.

Fast, Julius (1970). *Body language.* New York: Pocket Books.

Hall, Edward T. & Mildred Reed Hall (1990). *Understanding different cultures.* Yarmouth, Me.: Intercultural Press.

Morain, Genelle G. (1987). Kinesics and cross-cultural understanding. In Louise F. Luce & Elise C. Smith (eds.), *Toward internationalism: Readings in cross-cultural communication* (pp. 117–142). Cambridge, Mass.: Newbury House/Harper & Row. Now Boston: Heinle & Heinle.

Families, the Bedrock of Culture

4

INTRODUCTION

PREVIEW QUESTIONS

1. What are key differences in family structures and values around the world?
2. How do parents and children, wives and husbands relate to each other in various cultures?
3. How do women's and men's roles differ culturally?
4. How do children respond when faced with violence at home?
5. How can people create happier families, more balanced gender roles, and less violence?

Threads

My mother was dead for five years before I knew I loved her very much.

Writer Lillian Hellman

> Every family is a **miniature*** society,
> a social order with its own
> rules, structure, leadership,
> language, style of living.
>
> —*Arlene Skolnik and Jerome Skolnik*

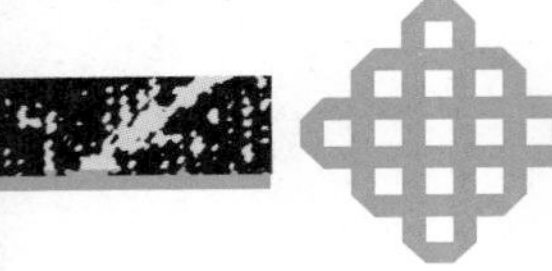

PATTERNS IN THIS CHAPTER

Families are the **bedrock** of culture. This chapter is about family structures and values, parents and children, wives and husbands. It is also about gender roles and about creating happier families. These are the key cultural patterns you should look for in this chapter.

We are all born into families, regardless of whether the families are as small as one parent or as big as 20 or 30 or 40 people—parents, siblings (brothers, sisters), cousins, aunts, uncles, grandparents, and so on. Here are a few important terms to understand:

- A *family* is traditionally defined as a group of people related by blood, marriage, or adoption.
- *Kinship* is the technical term for the bond they share.
- *Sex roles* are the roles men and women play, with an emphasis on the biological influences on behavior.
- *Gender roles* are the roles they play, stressing the cultural, rather than the biological, influences on behavior. Because this is a book about culture, the term *gender roles* is more appropriate here.

---

*Words in text set in bold type are listed aphabetically and defined in the Word Patterns section on page 133–134 of this chapter.

YOUR SUCCESS PATTERNS IN THIS CHAPTER

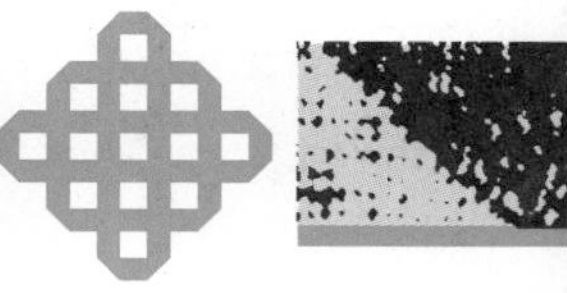

By the end of this chapter, using all four language skills, you will be able to:

- explain at least four key differences in family structures and values around the world;
- describe how parents and children interact in various cultures;
- explain how wives and husbands relate to each other in different cultures;
- tell how women's and men's roles differ culturally;
- describe how children respond when faced with violence at home;
- give hints on how to create happier families, more balanced gender roles, and less violence; and
- use many learning strategies to make your studying easier.

Task 4.1 Evaluating

THINKING ABOUT YOURSELF

IT WORKS! Learning Strategy: Assessing Your Ability

Step 1. Assess your current ability by circling the actions above that you can do *now.*

Step 2. Which actions did you *not* circle? These are the actions to which you can pay most attention in this chapter. (If you did not circle any of the actions listed above, then this is your golden opportunity to learn more about families as the basis of culture.)

CULTURAL PATTERN 1: FAMILY STRUCTURES AND VALUES

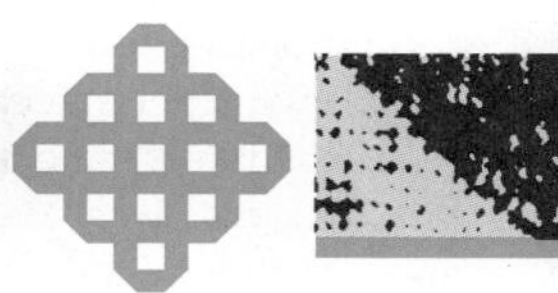

Task 4.2 Prereading

CONSIDERING TRADITIONAL CULTURES AND OTHER CULTURES

IT WORKS! Learning Strategy: Brainstorming

Brainstorm in a group: What are the signs of a traditional culture? What traditional cultures can you identify? (These signs and cultures become your hypotheses to be checked during the reading.)

Task 4.3 Reading

VERIFYING YOUR HYPOTHESES

IT WORKS!
Learning Strategy:
Checking Your Correctness

While reading, verify (check) your hypotheses from Task 4.2 to see if they are correct.

A few family structures and values around the globe

Families are the central core of our individual being and of our culture. Why is this so? Families give us our first concept of social reality. Families offer us our first view of the world. Families teach us that the world is kind or that it is cruel; that people are basically good or that they are mainly dangerous; and that we as little children are valuable or that we are worthless. Families provide us with our first values, which often become our lasting values. Families shape our thoughts and actions in untold ways, even if we rebel as teenagers.

The family is the center of most traditional Asians' lives. Many people worry about their families' welfare, reputation, and honor. Asian families are often extended, including several generations related by blood or marriage living in the same home. An Asian person's misdeeds are not blamed just on the individual but also on the family—including the dead ancestors.

Traditional Chinese, among many other Asians, respect their elders and feel a deep sense of duty toward them. Children repay their parents' sacrifices by being successful and supporting them in old age. This is accepted as a natural part of life in China. In contrast, taking care of aged parents is often viewed as a tremendous burden in the United States, where aging and family support are not honored highly. In fact, in the youth-oriented United States, growing old is seen as a bad thing, and many old people do not receive respect.

Filipinos, the most Americanized of the Asians, are still extremely family-oriented. They are dedicated to helping their children and will sacrifice greatly for their children to get an education. In turn, the children are devoted to their parents, who often live nearby. Grown children who go away and leave the country for economic reasons typically send large parts of their salary home to their parents and the rest of the family.

The Vietnamese family consists of people currently alive as well as the spirits of the dead and of the as-yet unborn. Any decisions or actions are done from family considerations, not individual desires. People's behavior is judged on whether it brings shame or pride to the family. The Vietnamese do not particularly believe in self-reliance; in this way, they are the opposite of people in the United States. Vietnamese children are trained to rely on their families, to honor elderly people, and to fear foreigners. Many Vietnamese think that their actions in this life will influence their status in the next life.

Fathers in traditional Japanese families are typically stern and aloof. Japanese college students in one study said they would tell their fathers just about as much as they would tell a total stranger. The emotional and communication barrier between children and fathers in Japan appears very strong after children have reached a certain age.

Traditional Latin Americans are as family-centered as the traditional Asians.

The family is the number one priority, the major frame of reference. Latin Americans believe that family members must help each other. Children in Latin America (of whom there are many, due to high fertility rates) are taught to respect authority and are given many responsibilities at home. The Latin American family emphasizes authority, with the males and older people being the most important. Responsibility is **delegated** based on age and sex. The family in most parts of Latin America includes many relatives, who remain in close contact. Family connections are the main way to get things done; dropping names (mentioning the names of important people the family knows) is often necessary to accomplish even simple things.

Although there has been much talk about "family values" in the United States, the family is not a usual frame of reference for decisions in U.S. mainstream culture. Family connections are not so important to most people. Dropping the names of wealthy or famous people the family knows is done in the United States, but it is not viewed positively. More important is a person's own individual "track record" of personal achievement.

Here you have seen a few different family structures and values around the world. In some cultures, the family is the center of life and the main frame of reference for decisions. In other cultures, the individual, not the family, is primary. In some cultures, the family's reputation and honor depend on each person's actions; in other cultures, individuals can act without permanently affecting the family itself. Some cultures value old people, while other cultures look down on them. Thus, many cultural differences exist in family structures and values.

A new slant on family values

LEARNING STRATEGY

Overcoming Limitations: Reading between the lines (inferring what is meant beyond what is actually said) is a useful way to overcome limitations.

Task 4.4 Postreading

COMPARING THE CULTURES

Step 1. Review the reading above. Also, think about what you already know from your own experience with families.

Step 2. Complete the chart by putting an "X" in each box that represents a value of the particular culture shown at the top of the column. Do not restrict your answers to what you have seen in this book; also use your own experience and background knowledge.

FAMILY VALUE	CULTURES			
	TRADITIONAL ASIAN	TRADITIONAL LATIN AMERICAN	U.S.	OTHER
Family members help each other.	____	____	____	____
Individuals go to institutions for help.	____	____	____	____
Old people are honored.	____	____	____	____
Old people are a source of wisdom.	____	____	____	____
Young people are the most important.	____	____	____	____
Everyone should look as young as possible.	____	____	____	____
It is important to sacrifice to give children whatever they need.	____	____	____	____
Children should stay with their parents until they are married.	____	____	____	____
Children should leave home as soon as they can become independent.	____	____	____	____
Mothers should have the final word.	____	____	____	____
Fathers should be **authoritarian.**	____	____	____	____

Step 3. Discuss your results with someone else. Do you see things the same way? If not, what are the differences? What role does your own background knowledge play in your responses?

Task 4.5 Expanding Your Knowledge

ANALYZING COMMON SAYINGS ABOUT FAMILIES

Sayings (including proverbs, everyday slogans, and comedy statements) often are short and sweet. They do not always explain everything fully. You will need to "read between the lines" to do this task.

Step 1. Read each of the sayings in Column 1.
Step 2. Write what you think it means in Column 2.
Step 3. In Column 3, write any cultural attitudes or assumptions that might underlie this saying.

EXAMPLE "The hand that rocks the cradle rules the world." This means: "The person who raises the children is the most important power in the whole world." The cultural assumption is that *mothers* (who usually raise children) can influence the way the world is run, and possibly that mothers are more important than fathers.

COLUMN 1 SAYING	COLUMN 2 DIRECT MEANING	COLUMN 3 CULTURAL ASSUMPTION
Blood is thicker than water.		
As the twig is bent, so grows the tree.		
That child is a chip off the old block.		
Spare the rod, spoil the child.		
Home is where the heart is.		
There's no place like home.		
Behind every successful man, there is a woman.		
A man might work from sun to sun, but a woman's work is never done.		
A woman's place is in the home.		
A woman's place is in the House—and in the Senate.		
That kid must have been born in a barn.		
No use crying over spilled milk.		
The way to a man's heart is through his stomach.		

Task 4.6 Prelistening

UNDERSTANDING LATIN AMERICAN FAMILIES

Discuss: Many Latin Americans believe that family is the most important aspect of life. Do you believe the same thing? Why or why not?

Task 4.7 Listening

COMPARING AND CONTRASTING

The title of this piece suggests that you will be comparing and contrasting two cultures. To do this, you could take notes in a three-part way, as shown below. Use a separate sheet of paper.

LEARNING STRATEGY

Forming Concepts: Making comparisons is a useful form of analysis that can help you understand an idea more quickly.

CHART OF FAMILY CHARACTERISTICS

CHARACTERISTICS		ADDITIONAL COMMENTS
MEXICAN FAMILIES	NORTH AMERICAN FAMILIES	

Your tape has **"The Supreme Importance of Families: Contrasts Between North Americans and Mexicans."** John Condon, *Good Neighbors: Communicating with the Mexicans,* reprinted with permission of Intercultural Press, Inc., Yarmouth, Me. Copyright 1985, pp. 23–25.

Task 4.8 Postlistening

PERSONALIZING THE EXPERIENCE

Step 1. Based on information about the family, what are the benefits of living in a Latin American country such as Mexico?
Step 2. Based on information about the family, what are the benefits of living in North America?
Step 3. How do these two cultures compare to your own in terms of families?
Step 4. Discuss your comments with someone else (from a different culture if possible).

IT WORKS! Learning Strategy: Linking with Your Own Experience

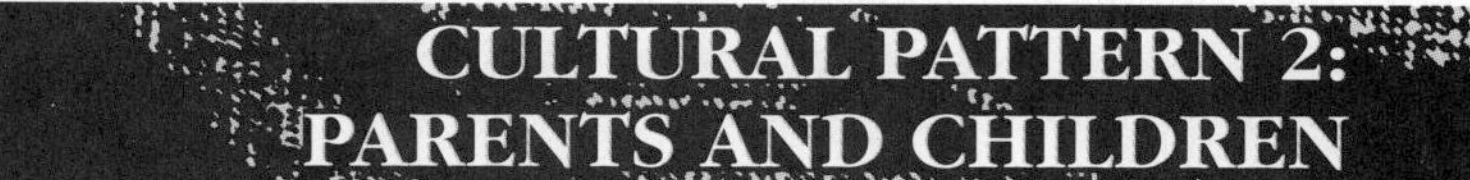

CULTURAL PATTERN 2: PARENTS AND CHILDREN

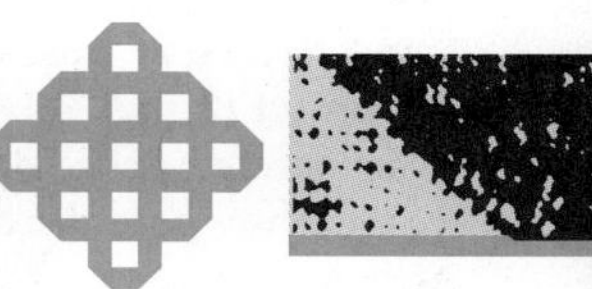

LEARNING STRATEGY

Forming Concepts: Writing things down quickly without criticizing them or correcting them ("quickwriting") can help generate new ideas for you.

Task 4.9 Prereading

PREDICTING WHAT JOHN MIGHT SAY

You will be reading a story by John L., a Vietnamese refugee to the United States. He wants his parents to be proud of him. Predict the ways he would like his parents to be proud of him. "Quickwrite" these ways. *Quickwriting* is like brainstorming, except you do it by yourself on paper. Write down anything that comes to your mind, without trying for accuracy.

Task 4.10 Reading

AVOIDING DISTRACTIONS AND LOOKING FOR THE MAIN IDEAS

As you read this piece, you might see a number of small grammatical problems. John has not mastered English perfectly. Do not become distracted by these errors; keep looking for the main ideas, which you can underline or jot down on a separate sheet.

I want my parents to be proud of me

by John L. (interviewed by Leah Zuch; grammar same as in original)

My parent say to me when I come to America, only one way to have good future is high education. When I come here my parent try to help me understand what to do, how to be successful. It is very hard because I didn't know any English and my parent just know some. My family want me to do good, to do very well, and I want them to be proud of me. You have to listen to your parent, any advice they tell you. I respect my parent because they work very hard to always have good thing for me and my sisters. I'm the only son in my family, so it's my responsibility to do good and to protect them if I have to. You have to have money, and you have to be strong. When I have money I will help my parent—you can't do anything without enough money.

My parent teach me honesty, pride in our culture and family, and that good education is necessary. Always do the good thing, not the bad thing, and good thing will come to you. When you work hard, study hard, you will get the good thing, never do the way very cheap. When you work hard and earn money by yourself you will feel good, feel proud. They advise me to be friends with honest person.

I feel sad for my father [former official in the Vietnamese government]. In Vietnam he had very hard time in prison, only one meal a day and that food was very bad. He had to stay in jail for ten year and almost die. My mother used to take my sisters and me to see him and bring him food. It was very far to go from Saigon north to border of Vietnam and China. The Communists were cruel to my father, sometime they put him in a box, very small, with no light, no food. He only live because he used to be very strong man. He practiced Kung Fu and has black belt like me but he is sometime better than me. He's still strong, even now he sometime beat me when we practice. He's very tough teacher! His experience in the prison make him very quiet, very shy, but he still very tough. He's very smart and know how to survive bad thing. I think he is very good man.

My mother [who has a master's degree in political science from Vietnam] worked hard to help us live when my father was in prison. She also very smart and knows what to do, how to survive the Communist government. They put her in jail too in 1975, but let her go home after one year because she has three children. She had to give money to Communists, yes a **bribe,** so we could stay in our house and for many other thing we need. She and my father are very happy to be in the United States. She said to me when we came, "Freedom, John. I'm happy now because we have freedom!" I like that too, but sometime after I finish my education I will return to Asia. Not Vietnam, I hate Communist, but maybe Japan. I love Japan.

Task 4.11 Postreading

COMPARING JOHN'S VALUES WITH THE VALUES YOUR PARENTS TAUGHT YOU

Step 1. What are at least three main values John's parents taught him?
Step 2. What are at least three important values your parents taught you?
Step 3. Are there any cultural differences in these two sets of values? Explain.
Step 4. Why do you believe John hates the Communists so much?
Step 5. Do you think he might change his mind and visit Vietnam again? Why or why not?

Task 4.12 Prelistening

CONSIDERING WHAT YOU KNOW ALREADY

Brainstorm: What do you know about Black families in North America? What are some of the pressures and difficulties they face? What are some of their strengths?

LEARNING STRATEGY

Remembering New Material: Taking notes on names and characteristics helps you remember people.

Task 4.13 Listening

SEEKING OUT THE NAMES AND FEATURES

While listening, write down the *names* of the women or girls in the three generations of this family. Write down *at least one important feature or characteristic* of each of these people.

Your tape has **"Three Generations of Single Mothers,"** by Michelle Ingrassia. From *Newsweek,* Aug. 30, 1993, p. 25, and

Mother and daughter

Task 4.14 Postlistening

BREAKING THE CYCLE

Step 1. Describe the generation-after-generation cycle that you heard about in this story.
Step 2. Do the mother and grandmother feel this cycle can be broken? Explain.
Step 3. What suggestions do you have to break the cycle?

Task 4.15 Prereading

CONSIDERING THE BACKGROUND

Discuss: Where is Cuba? What is the government like in Cuba? Why did many Cubans emigrate to the United States?

Task 4.16 Reading

DISTINGUISHING BETWEEN GENERATIONS

As you read, write down the differences between father and son in their attitudes and interests.

Father oriented toward Cuba, son toward America

by David Rieff

In families with younger kids still living at home, the outlines of the bargain that had been struck between the adults who spoke of Cuba and the children who watched Miami Heat games were even clearer. [Coral Gables architect] Raul Rodriguez's office was decorated with images of Havana and his work. In Raul and Ninon's bedroom at home, there were portraits of the family on the dresser and a stack of books on Cuba by the bed . . . .

But in Ruly's [the son's] room, there were only the icons of an American 12-year-old from a prosperous family: posters of sports stars—the basketball player Michael Jordan caught in mid-leap, an old-timey image of Lou Gehrig of the 1920s-era New York Yankees—as well as a basic Apple computer, a poster reading "I like my room this way," and a Nintendo system.

But if the conversations in the living room were so often in Spanish and about Cuba, it was possible, in the moments when the talk died down, to hear the blare of the television broadcasting a ballgame from Ruly's room, to hear the boy talking, in English naturally, with his friends, or to have him come running out to announce to Raul, "Dad, the Yankees just scored two runs," or "Dad, you should have seen the catch Canseco just made!"

At those moments, Raul would shake himself out of the **exile** mind-set from which he had been operating, put aside the questions over which he had been arguing with his wife and his guests . . . and become again, for a time, a doting Cuban-American father. He might insist, over Ruly's objections, that the boy make the trips to Cuba, but at home in Miami Raul watched his son grow up American and, those visits aside, made no attempt to arrest the process.

Source: David Rieff, The Exile: Cuba in the Heart of Miami. New York: Simon & Schuster, 1993; reprinted in the Miami Herald, August 8, 1993, pp. 1C and 4C.

Task 4.17 Postreading

BRIDGING THE GAP

Step 1. Look at your notes from the reading. What are the main differences between son Ruly and father Raul in terms of their attitudes and interests?

Step 2. What is meant by "exile mind-set"? You might have to go beyond the reading a little bit.

Step 3. How does Raul try to bridge the gap between himself and his son?

Task 4.18 Prelistening

THINKING ABOUT WORRIES

On a big sheet of paper, make a list of things that parents worry about concerning their young children. On a second sheet of paper, make a list of things that adult children worry about regarding their aging parents.

Task 4.19 Listening

UNDERSTANDING TWO POEMS WITH DIFFERENT POINTS OF VIEW

As you listen, notice the worries of the mothers in the first poem. Hear the concerns of the son in the second poem.

Your tape has **"Parents Worry About Their Children and Vice Versa."** Excerpt from "The Child Bearers," *45 Mercy Street* by Anne Sexton. Copyright © 1976 by Linda Gray Sexton and Loring Conant, Jr. Reprinted by permission of Houghton Mifflin Co. All right reserved.

Your tape also has "Point Sur," *Doublespace*, pp. 81–82. Copyright © 1992 by Hank Lazer. Reprinted by permission of the Segue Foundation, New York.

Father and son

Task 4.20 Postlistening

COMPARING CONCERNS

IT WORKS! Learning Strategy: Examining Others' Feelings

Step 1. What are the concerns of the mothers in the poem "The Child Bearers"? Are these concerns specific or general?

Step 2. What are the concerns of the son in the poem "Point Sur"? Are these concerns specific or general?

Step 3. What are some similarities between these two poems (for instance, the quality of love)?

Step 4. What are some differences between these two poems?

Task 4.21 Prereading

MEDITATING ABOUT MOTHERS

IT WORKS! Learning Strategy: Brainstorming

With others, brainstorm the best qualities you would like to have in a mother. Make the list as long as possible. Make sure everyone in your group has a copy of the list.

Task 4.22 Reading

The mother

COMPARING THE IDEAL WITH REALITY

As you read, use the list from the previous task to check off the good qualities of the mother in this story. Add any other good qualities that you did not have on your initial list.

A special kind of mother

by Banana Yoshimoto

Just then, with the scratch of a key in the door, an incredibly beautiful woman came running in, all out of breath.

I was so stunned, I gaped. Though she didn't seem young, she was truly beautiful. From her outfit and dramatic makeup, which really wouldn't do for daytime, I understood that hers was night work.

Yuichi introduced me: "This is Mikage Sakurai."

"How do you do," she said in a slightly husky voice, still panting, with a smile. "I'm Yuichi's mother. My name is Eriko."

This was his mother? Dumbfounded, I couldn't take my eyes off her. Hair that rustled like silk to her shoulders; the deep sparkle of her long, narrow eyes; well-formed lips, a nose with a high, straight bridge—the whole of her gave off a marvelous light that seemed to vibrate with life force. She didn't look human. I had never seen anyone like her.

I was staring to the point of rudeness. "How do you do," I replied at last, smiling back at her.

"We're so pleased to have you here," she said to me warmly, and then, turning to Yuichi, "I'm sorry, Yuichi. I just can't get away tonight. I dashed out for a second saying that I was off to the bathroom. But I'll have plenty of time in the morning. I hope Mikage will agree to spend the night." She was in a rush and ran to the door, red dress flying.

. . . She was stunning. She made me want to be with her again. There was a warm light, like her afterimage, slowly glowing in my heart. That must be what they mean by "charm." Like Helen Keller when she understood "water" for the first time, the word burst into reality for me, its living example before my eyes. It's no **exaggeration;** the encounter was that overwhelming.

. . . "Mikage," he said, "were you a little bit intimidated by my mother?"

"Yes," I told him frankly. "I've never seen a woman that beautiful."

"Yes. But . . ." Smiling, he sat down on the floor right in front of me. "She's had plastic surgery."

"Oh?" I said, feigning nonchalance. "I wondered why she didn't look anything like you."

"And that's not all. Guess what else—she's a man." He could barely contain his amusement.

This was too much. I stared at him in wide-eyed silence. I expected any second he would say, "Just kidding." Those tapered fingers, those **mannerisms,** the way she carried herself . . . I held my breath remembering that beautiful face; he, on the other hand, was enjoying this.

"Yes, but . . ." My mouth hung open. "You've been saying all along, 'my mother' this, 'my mother' that. . . ."

"Yes, but. Could *you* call someone who looked like that 'Dad'?" he asked calmly.

. . . "What about the name Eriko?"

"It's actually Yuji."

It was as though there were a haze in front of my eyes. When I was finally ready to hear the story, I said, "So, who gave birth to you?"

"Eriko was a man a long time ago. He married very young. The person he married was my mother. . . . As a child Eriko [Yuji] was taken in by her family. I don't know why. They grew up together. Even as a man he was good-looking, and apparently he was very popular with women . . . . He must have been pretty attached to my mother. So much that he turned his back on the debt of gratitude he owed his foster parents and eloped with her."

I nodded.

"After my real mother died, Eriko quit her job, gathered me up, and asked herself, 'What do I want to do now?' What she decided was, 'Become a woman.' She knew she'd never love anybody else. She says that before she became a woman she was very shy. Because she hates to do things halfway, she had everything 'done,' from her face to her whatever, and with the money she had left over she bought that nightclub. She raised me a woman alone, as it were." He smiled.

"What an *amazing* life story!"

"She's not dead yet," said Yuichi.

* * *

"It's not easy being a woman," said Eriko one evening, out of the blue.

I lifted my nose from the magazine I was reading and said, "Huh?" The beautiful Eriko was watering the plants in front of the terrace before she left for work.

"Because I have a lot of faith in you, I suddenly feel I ought to tell you something. I learned it raising Yuichi. There were many, many difficult times, god knows. If a person wants to stand on her own two feet, I recommend undertaking the care and feeding of something. It could be children, or it could be house plants, you know? By doing that you come to understand your own limitations. That's where it starts." As if chanting a **liturgy,** she related to me her philosophy of life.

"Life can be so hard," I said, moved.

"Yes. But if a person hasn't ever experienced true despair, she grows old never knowing how to evaluate where she is in life; never understanding what joy really is. I'm grateful for it." . . . Enveloped in the twilight coming from the west, there she was, watering the plants with her slender, graceful hands, in the midst of a light so sweet it seemed to form a rainbow in the transparent water she poured.

Task 4.23 Postreading

GETTING OVER THE SURPRISE

Step 1. What was your greatest surprise about the mother in this story?
Step 2. Did that surprise cause you to be prejudiced against (or for) the mother? Explain.
Step 3. How many good qualities did you find for the mother? What were those qualities?
Step 4. Would you like to have a mother like this? Explain.
Step 5. Do you think Yuichi was happy? Give evidence from the story.
Step 6. On a separate page, write a story of your own about a good mother. Share it with at least two other people.

CULTURAL PATTERN 3: MARRIAGE

Task 4.24 Prelistening

LOOKING FOR A MATE

Quickwrite all the qualities you would look for in a mate. (If you are already married, indicate the qualities you like in your mate.)

Task 4.25 Listening

SEEKING THE THREE MAIN QUALITIES

As you listen, try to find the three main criteria people usually use for choosing a mate. Also consider whether arranged marriages are good.

Your tape has **"Choosing Mates,"** which contains some concepts adapted from William Kornblum, *Sociology in a Changing World,* New York: Holt, Rinehart and Winston, 1988.

Choosing mates

Task 4.26 Postlistening

ANALYZING THE DATA

Step 1. List the three main criteria for choosing mates in most cultures.
Step 2. Circle the criteria in Step 1 that are used for choosing mates in your culture. Now add any others below that your culture usually uses:
Step 3. What are the advantages of arranged marriages?
Step 4. What are the advantages of marriages that are decided by the couple, not arranged by the parents or community?

Task 4.27 Prereading

CONSIDERING WHEN MARRIAGE BEGAN

Brainstorm with others: When did marriage begin? Why did it begin?

LEARNING STRATEGY

Understanding and Using Emotions: Using your physical senses helps you understand both emotions and ideas.

Task 4.28 Reading

NOTICING COLD AND HEAT

In this poem, notice the cold and heat. Write down or circle any mention of cold and any mention of heat.

Marriage

Marriage is not
a house or even a tent

it is before that, and colder:

the edge of the forest, the edge
of the desert
the unpainted stairs
at the back where we squat
outside, eating popcorn

the edge of the receding glacier

where painfully and with wonder
at having survived even
this far

we are learning to make fire

—Margaret Atwood

Task 4.29 Postreading

FEELING THE CHILL AND THE WARMTH

Step 1. Why might marriage be cold, and what images of cold does the poet use?
Step 2. What specific historical image of the Ice Age does the poet employ?
Step 3. What does the poet mean by "we are learning to make fire"?
Step 4. Is this poem optimistic or pessimistic? Explain your reasons.

Task 4.30 Prelistening

CONTRASTING IDEAS OF DIVORCE

Discuss (in a multicultural group if possible): Is divorce acceptable in your society? How does your culture look at divorced people? What percentage of people in your society are divorced?

Task 4.31 Listening

KEEPING TRACK OF WHO'S WHO

While listening, keep a written record of who's who in each family. (You will need it later!)

Your tape has **"Friend Maria Elena and I Have Different Views About Divorce,"** by Michael Chrismartin. Used with permission.

Task 4.32 Postlistening

MAKING FAMILY TREES

Step 1. Examine this family tree showing Mike's four families.

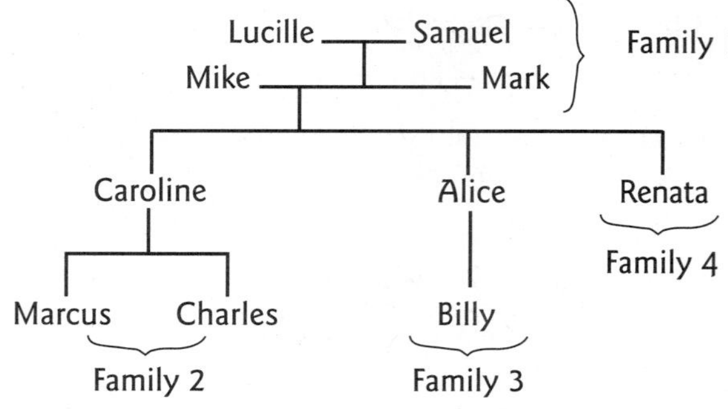

Mike's family tree

Step 2. Create a family tree for Maria Elena. You can put Rodolfo and Maria Elena on the same line, since there have been no other spouses. Underneath, put the four children. Be sure to draw lines to show "kinship."

Step 3. Now draw your family tree. Start with your grandparents, then your parents, then your generation (including sisters, brothers, spouses), then any children from that generation. Make sure to draw lines to show the relationships.

LEARNING STRATEGY

Forming Concepts: Debating about an issue helps clarify your views in a systematic way.

Task 4.33 Expanding Your Knowledge

DEBATING ABOUT DIVORCE

Step 1. Conduct research on divorce in different cultures. Find at least five different ways that cultures deal with divorce.

Step 2. Take a side in a debate about whether children should be allowed to "divorce" their parents, as has happened recently in the United States. (You could also have a debate about whether parents should be allowed to divorce each other.)

Step 3. The person or team with the strongest argument (supported by the best evidence) wins the debate.

Task 4.34 Prereading

THINKING ABOUT ABUSE

Discuss the following in a mixed-culture group: What if a husband **abuses** a wife physically or mentally? Is this okay? What if a wife does the same to the husband?

Task 4.35 Reading

CONSIDERING WHAT YOU WOULD DO

As you read, think about what you would personally do if you were in Sylvia's situation. Write down ideas.

The worst kind of abuse

by Sylvia F.

I was born in Goa, India, as one of three children. My family has mixed Indian and Portuguese blood. Many Portuguese had settled in my part of India at one time, bringing with them the Catholic religion. My whole family is Catholic, and I have a strong Catholic faith. This faith has saved my sanity and life.

My father died when I was young. I grew up in a family that included my mother, my sister Mavis, and my brother Tony. These names are typical of my region of India, where English is commonly spoken along with Gujarati. My mother supported the family. She sent me to an English-speaking Catholic school. The nuns liked me because I had athletic ability. I won regional and national trophies for basketball and track, until I damaged my knee in a competition. I also did well in academic classes.

I decided to take business courses. After graduating and saying goodbye to the beloved nuns (I still hear from some of them years later!), I took a job as a secretary and administrative assistant in a Bombay office. My boss was handsome and charming. His name was R. Despite the difference in religion, we fell in love after working together closely for months. Soon we were married.

Almost immediately, R., my new husband, decided to move to the United States, where he felt business would be more profitable. We moved to the state of Virginia, near Washington, D.C. Suddenly he didn't want me to work outside the home any more. He only permitted me to go out with him to the grocery store once per week, and he drove; I was not allowed to learn to drive. My independent ways were no longer okay.

R. allowed me to work at tailoring and sewing clothes in the apartment, but that was all. Fortunately, I had a natural talent for this kind of work. I could remember measurements without writing them down and could see at a glance just how much fabric needed to be taken up or let out. With good advertising, my at-home business was soon thriving. I made many friends among the customers who came to the apartment.

Meanwhile, R.'s business was not doing well. He moved from one business idea to the next, never putting enough time or energy into it to make a success of anything. He became envious that I was so successful and had so many friends. At the same time, I was pregnant with our first child and soon afterwards our second, both girls. This put financial stress on the family, and such stress made R. even angrier. He took his rage out on me through verbal and physical abuse while the children watched.

R.'s family never approved of my Catholicism or Christianity in general, so they never accepted me as R.'s proper wife. They wanted R. to marry a woman of his own religion. R. disliked my religious faith. Whenever his Indian family visited the United States from their adopted country, England, they created problems about the religious difference.

One day, after R.'s anger and envy got hot, he told me he was taking the children to the K-Mart to buy them shoes. He grabbed the girls, one 3 and one 2, both barefooted, and whisked them into the car. Instead of taking them to the K-Mart, he took them to Dulles International Airport, from which they flew to England to be with his parents. I never saw the two children again. I hired British detectives and lawyers to search for R. and the children, but every time these professionals got close, R. moved the girls to a new town. Then he found another woman, and together they took the girls to France, where they were lost to the detectives and lawyers for good.

My life changed entirely as a result of this. For the first six months after the kidnapping, I was so depressed that I could do nothing but pray to the Virgin Mary and work on clients' sewing and tailoring. I could not laugh, and I could hardly talk. I prayed for the courage to continue living, even though I thought of suicide. After six months, my strength came back. Finally I bought a car, took driving lessons, and got a job as a tailor at an expensive, well-known department store. After a year I obtained a divorce.

I continued praying at my little candle-lit shrine of the Virgin Mary, and I started going to one of the local Catholic churches. At my job I was promoted several times. I was then transferred to Chicago as the supervisor of dozens of tailors in the same department store chain. I recently bought my own home in Chicago.

I recognize my children's birthdays, pray for them, and sometimes look at their old photographs hanging on the wall. The only way I can deal with this great loss is to keep close contact with God and to work as hard as I can.

Task 4.36 Postreading

CHECKING YOUR UNDERSTANDING AND YOUR EMOTIONS

Step 1. Why was R. angry at his wife, Sylvia? Give at least three reasons.
Step 2. What problems did R. have that he blamed on Sylvia?
Step 3. What role did R.'s parents play in the situation?
Step 4. What did R. do to punish Sylvia?
Step 5. What were her responses?
Step 6. How would you have handled things if you were Sylvia?
Step 7. What cultural influences might affect your responses?
Step 8. Discuss your answers with someone else.

Threads

There's sex and there's marriage, and the two have absolutely nothing in common.

Attributed to the father of John F. Kennedy

CULTURAL PATTERN 4: WOMEN'S AND MEN'S ROLES IN FAMILIES (AND OUTSIDE)

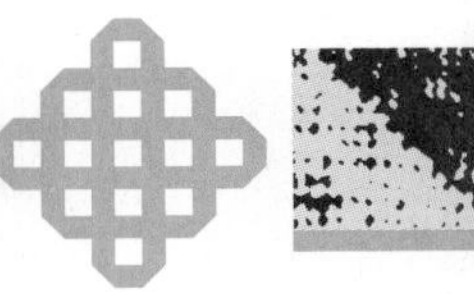

Task 4.37 Prelistening

DEFINING THE TERMS

Discuss: What is "the battle between the sexes"? Have you fought this battle in your own life? Have you seen others fight it? Is it real or imaginary?

Task 4.38 Listening

DETERMINING WHETHER YOU AGREE

The author, Roger Axtell, says some controversial things about the battle between the sexes. Take notes as you listen. Then put a check beside each point with which you agree.

Your tape has **"Battle of the Sexes Continues,"** by Roger Axtell, from *Do's and Taboos Around the World,* 3rd ed. New York: John Wiley, pp. 22–25.

Task 4.39 Postlistening

CHECKING THE TRUTH FACTOR

Step 1. Circle TRUE or FALSE. Rely on *your own knowledge,* not just what the author tells you.

a. Women are often found in places of power within America.	TRUE	FALSE
b. Women have the same rights as men in America.	TRUE	FALSE
c. Women have as much power as men in Western Europe.	TRUE	FALSE
d. Women can easily eat alone at restaurants throughout Europe.	TRUE	FALSE
e. Women cannot drive in Saudi Arabia.	TRUE	FALSE
f. Women who serve as geishas are prostitutes.	TRUE	FALSE
g. Women in China have full power to govern.	TRUE	FALSE
h. Women in Buddhist and Muslim countries sometimes cannot mix with men socially.	TRUE	FALSE
i. Women in Latin America and the Philippines can work in high places in business and government.	TRUE	FALSE
j. Women who appear pushy are accepted well in most cultures.	TRUE	FALSE

Step 2. Do your answers completely agree with the statements made by the author? If not, explain.

Step 3. Compare your answers with those of other people. Note any cultural differences.

Task 4.40 Prereading

EXPLORING OPPRESSION

Discuss with others: What does **oppression** mean? How is it possible for one person to be oppressed by another? How often does it happen? Is there such a thing as oppression of women?

Threads

Nobody objects to a woman being a good writer or sculptor or geneticist if at the same time she is a good wife, a good mother, good looking, good tempered, well dressed, well groomed, and unaggressive.

Writer Marya Mannes

Task 4.41 Reading

CITING INSTANCES OF OPPRESSION

As you read the two pieces, one serious and the other tongue-in-cheek, count the number of examples of oppression that you find. Highlight them with a star or underline them.

The historical view of women's oppression is by Mary Livermore, and the science fiction approach is by Suzette Haden Elgin. Both suggest similar concepts.

Female oppression

by Mary Livermore

No one who has studied history, even **superficially,** will for a moment dispute the statement that . . . there has brooded very steadily over the female half of the human family an air of repression, of limitation, of hindrance, of disability, of gloom, of **servitude.** If there have been epochs during which women have been regarded equal to men, they have been brief and abnormal.

. . . Among the Hindus, woman was the slave of man, forbidden to speak the language of her master, and compelled to use the patois [speech] of the slaves. The Hebrews pronounced her an afterthought of the Deity, and the mother of all evil. The Greek law regarded her as a child, and held her in life-long **tutelage.** The Greek philosophers proclaimed her a "monster," "an accidental production." Medieval councils declared her unfit for instruction. The early Christian fathers denounced her as a "**noxious** animal," a "painted **temptress,**" a "necessary evil," "a desirable calamity," a "domestic peril."

. . . In marriage she has been a **serf;** as a mother she has been robbed of her children; in public instruction she has been ignored; in labor she has been a **menial,** and then inadequately compensated; civilly she has been a minor, and politically she has had no existence. She has been the equal of man only when punishment and the payment of taxes were in question.

Source: Mary Livermore, Lecture, 1867. Public domain.

Reducing women to their correct status

by Suzette Haden Elgin

Scholars acknowledge the magnificent research of Haskyl and Netherland which proved the genetic inferiority of the human female. They admit it was the prompt and efficient male response to Haskyl and Netherland's work, at every level of government, which brought about the speedy passage in 1991 of the constitutional amendments restoring women to their proper and valuable place in society [women's status = children to be cared for by men], and formally imposing upon men the stewardship role so many had neglected for at least the preceding fifty years. But they persist—with an almost feminine disregard for the requirements of scholarship—in their claim that prior to Haskyl and Netherland the twentieth century was a scientific wasteland, in which no research or publication in **feminology** can be found . . . . This is manifestly absurd.

. . . The most cursory viewing of collections [of commercial advertisements from the twentieth century] demonstrates that although lip service to "feminist" views was paid by what might be referred to as the *intellectual* media, no such distortion existed elsewhere . . . . Those with *true* power—for example, those who controlled the advertising industry, the giant corporations, the health care industry, the national defense, and the major churches—were clearly quite free of such [feminist] ignorance.

Any scholar who reads the records of history from about 1940 to 1990 with *care* finds an abundance of examples stating both the inferiority of the female and the custodial obligations of the male. This is true even when the curious social customs of the time necessitate various mechanisms for disguising those principles, as opposed to stating them openly . . . .

Source: Suzette Haden Elgin, The Judas Rose: Native Tongue II. New York: DAW Books, Inc., 1987, pp. 49–50. Used with permission.

Task 4.42 Postreading

ANALYZING WHAT YOU READ

Step 1. List at least five negative labels women have been given by men, as seen in the two readings.

Step 2. How have women been treated at home and in public life, according to Mary Livermore and Suzette Haden Elgin? Give five examples.

Step 3. Was the feminist movement of the late 1900s taken seriously by business, health care, churches, and government (see Elgin)? Explain.

Step 4. What did Haskyl and Netherland do to promote the passage of the (hypothetical) 1991 amendment to reduce women to the status of children?

Step 5. What is your opinion about the 1991 amendment? Do you consider it fair to men and women? What kind of changes, if any, might you make in that amendment?

CULTURE CLIP!
Running the Show, Pressing the Buttons, Making the Money

. . . Old men run things. Old men run the show, press the buttons, make the wars, make the money. In the man's world, the old man's world, the young men run and run and run until they drop, and some of the young women run with them. But old women live in the cracks, between the walls, like roaches, like mice, a rustling sound, a squeaking. Better lock up the cheese, boys. It's terrible, you turn up a corner of civilization and there are all these old women running around on the wrong side . . . .

Listen to other women, your sisters, your mothers, your grandmothers —if you don't hear them, how will you ever understand what your daughter says to you?

Now this is what I want: I want to hear your judgments. I am sick of the silence of women. I want to hear you speaking all the languages, offering your experience as your truth, as human truth, talking about working, about making, about unmaking, about eating, about cooking, about feeding, about taking in seed and giving out life, about killing, about feeling, about thinking; about what women do; about what men do; about war, about peace; about who presses the buttons and what buttons get pressed and whether pressing buttons is in the long run a fit occupation for human beings. There's a lot of things I want to hear you talk about.

Source: Ursula Le Guin, Bryn Mawr College Commencement Address, 1986, in Dancing at the Edge of the World: Thoughts on Words, Women, Places. Copyright © 1989 Grove/Atlantic, Inc., pp. 147–190.

Threads

The roosters may crow, but the hens deliver the eggs.

Politician Dianne Feinstein

Think! Does this picture describe your native culture? Does it describe other cultures? With which aspects of the picture do you agree? With which aspects do you disagree?

Task 4.43 Prelistening

GETTING READY FOR THE PHYSICAL

Prepare yourself for hearing about physical oppression. Some of it is not pretty. Discuss: What kind of physical oppression against women might you predict from your own background knowledge?

Task 4.44 Listening

SEPARATING MORE SERIOUS FROM LESS SERIOUS OPPRESSIONS

While reading, write the more serious oppressions in one column and the less serious oppressions (if any) in another column. This helps you be a "critical listener."

Your tape has **"Physical Oppression of Women."**

A corset is a good way to restrict a woman's activity.

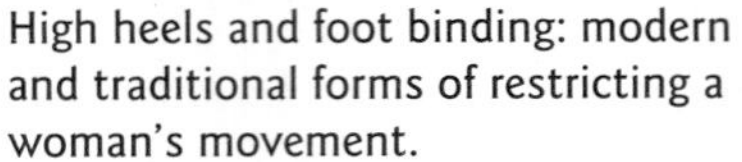

High heels and foot binding: modern and traditional forms of restricting a woman's movement.

Task 4.45 Postlistening

LISTING THE PHYSICAL OPPRESSIONS

Step 1. List all the forms of physical oppression and domination of women found in this reading.
Step 2. Which of these are more serious, and which are less serious? Discuss with someone else.
Step 3. Now list other forms of physical oppression and domination found in your culture that have not been mentioned here.
Step 4. Add to the list by talking with people from other cultures about oppression of women in their cultures.
Step 5. Speculate on why women have received such abuse for so long.
Step 6. Consider the changes that would take place if women in large numbers rebelled against such physical oppression.

Task 4.46 Expanding Your Knowledge

SPIKING THOSE HEELS

Step 1. Discuss the following questions:

a. How do you feel about fashion as an oppressor of women (or of men)?
b. Do you think that spike heels hurt women in any way?
c. Are there any other female fashions that might be harmful or oppressive?
d. Are there any current fashions for men in various cultures that bind, constrict, or harm men?
e. Are there any current fashions that cause men pain?
f. If so, what are these?
g. Why would men wear them?

Step 2. Conduct research on the history of fashion and find out all you can about the psychology of clothing. Discover why people wear what they do. Find out what hurts and what does not—as seen through the ages of history. Discover times and cultures in which men wore high heels!

LEARNING STRATEGY

Forming Concepts: Looking at concepts historically or developmentally can help you see important changes.

Task 4.47 Expanding Your Knowledge

COMPARING GENDER ROLES HISTORICALLY

Step 1. In your notebook write the title "Traditional Gender Roles." Make two columns: MEN and WOMEN. In the appropriate column, write words or phrases that describe what is expected in "traditional" roles of men and of women.

Step 2. In your notebook write the title "Changes in Gender Roles." Make two columns: MEN and WOMEN. In the appropriate column, write words or phrases that show changes in the gender roles of men and women in recent years—or changes you hope will occur.

Step 3. Discuss your results with someone else, preferably from another culture. Do you see eye-to-eye on traditional gender roles? Do you agree about changes in gender roles?

Threads

It is easier to rule a kingdom than to regulate a family.

Japanese proverb

LEARNING STRATEGY

Overcoming Limitations: Considering carefully the things that make you uncomfortable—things you would ordinarily choose to ignore—can help you learn to accept your culture and other cultures.

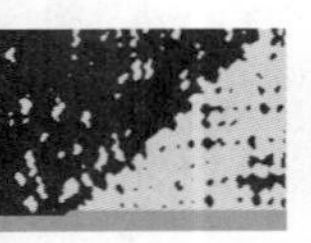

CULTURAL PATTERN 5: CHILDREN FACE VIOLENCE AT HOME

Task 4.48 Prereading

Threads

The secret cruelties that parents visit upon their children are past belief.

Dr. Karl A. Menninger

CONSIDERING THE PROBLEMS

Answer these questions with YES or NO:

- Is family violence a problem in the United States? ________
- Is family violence a problem in many other cultures? ________
- Is family violence a problem in your culture? ________

Task 4.49 Reading

IT WORKS! Learning Strategy: Guessing from Context

IDENTIFYING PROBLEMS AND SOLUTIONS

As you read, list all the problems that you encounter. Also list any solutions that the family used, successfully or not, to solve those problems. Use guessing to help you with any difficult words.

When violence hits home

by U.S. Representative Dan Burton

One of my earliest memories is of being awakened in the early morning hours by a terrible noise. I was 5 or 6 years old and my father, mother, younger sister, and I were living in a duplex house in Indianapolis. I heard the sound of furniture being shoved across the room and a lamp crashing to the floor. Then I heard my mother's bloodcurdling scream. Every nerve in my body stood on end. Terrified, I lay there thinking, "My God, it's happening again."

For almost a decade, my father beat my mother nearly every week. Anything seemed to set him off: jealousy, rage over something that hadn't gone his way. He'd start by saying horrible things to her. He'd rip her clothes off and throw her down. Sometimes he literally knocked her unconscious. Afterward, her face and eyes would be swollen and bruised. He'd put wet cloths on her face to wake her up. I'd hear him consoling her, saying he was sorry, that it would never happen again. But of course it did.

Dan Burton

Sometimes I'd try to stop him. I remember going partway down the stairs and yelling, "Stop, stop!" but my father would say, "Get back upstairs." Physically, there was nothing I could do. My mother would scream and holler for help, but nobody ever came. I was afraid to tell anyone. I thought my father would attack me.

Dad was 6'8" and a **vicious** guy. I don't think he was born mean, but when he was growing up he was picked on by other kids. But after he learned to fight back, he realized that he was strong enough to inflict pain—and so he used that to his advantage. It carried over into his marriage and his family.

Dad wasn't dumb, but he was a vagabond. He never held a job for very long. We lived a ragtag existence, moving from trailer parks to cabins to motels. By the time I was 12, we had lived in 38 states, in Mexico and in Canada. I remember once enrolling in school in the morning, only to move in the afternoon.

Mother wasn't the only object of his violence. She told me about a time when I was 6 months old; my parents took me to the movies, and I started crying, as babies will do. He took me out to the lobby. Later my mother saw that I was black and blue from my shoulders to my ankles. Another beating, I remember vividly, took place when I was 10. We were living in a small motel in Niles, Mich. Dad gave me a list of groceries and ordered me to go to a little store a few blocks away. It was snowing like crazy when I started back to the motel with the groceries. The bags got wet and broke, spilling the groceries everywhere. I gathered up whatever I could carry in my hands. When I got back, my father beat the hell out of me. He was embarrassed to have to go pick the groceries up out of the snow.

I was so terrified of him I would try to stay out of his way as much as possible. When things got really bad, my mother would sit me down and read inspirational poems aloud. Occasionally she would move out. She'd take us and go to her relatives, but she was afraid to leave him for good. He threatened to come after her if she ever did. In those days, there were no shelters where battered women could go for safety. There was no place to hide. The beatings got worse. Finally my mother decided that if she didn't leave, he would kill one of us. In 1950, when I was 12, she went to the police and got a restraining order, then moved us to her mother's house on Division Street in Indianapolis. It was a very small old house with no indoor plumbing. I slept in one twin bed with my brother. My mother and sister slept in another.

A few months later, my father made good on his threat. He broke into the house through an attic window. I remember him kicking the bedroom door open. He had a sawed-off shotgun and dragged my mother away. I had a baseball bat next to my bed, but it happened so fast I couldn't do anything.

For several days we didn't know if she was dead or alive. Because my grandmother was too old to take care of us on her own, law enforcement authorities placed us in the Marion County Guardian Home. My mother managed to escape when Dad pulled the car over to get some sleep. He had taken the knobs off the doors and windows on the passenger side, but somehow she managed to climb over him and get out. He was arrested and charged with kidnapping. I remember being called to testify at his trial. The **prosecutor** told me, "You don't have to be afraid now," but when I saw Dad sitting there I was scared to death. He went to jail for two years.

My mother divorced him and later remarried. My new stepfather was a wonderful man. He only made $75 a week before taxes working at a foundry in Indianapolis, but he took us into his house and gave us love and guidance. He never resorted to physical punishment. When we would get rowdy, he'd just tell us to simmer down. For the first time, I felt safe.

. . . I know that violence is a *learned* response. People who have been abused as children often end up abusing their own wives and children. Growing up, I had a tendency to lash out too when I was angry. Fortunately, my mother and grandmother helped me with love, kindness, and encouragement. When I got married and had my own family, I made a conscious effort to control my anger because I recall what it was like in that house.

I also learned that unless an abusive man gets professional help, he is not going to change. He may make promises for a few weeks, but then it will start all over again. My message to women with abusive husbands is to get out. It was only when my mother escaped my father that we could begin to live a normal, productive life.

Source: U.S. Representative Dan Burton, in People Weekly, April 4, 1994, pp. 91–96. Reprinted by permission of People Weekly.

Task 4.50 Postlistening

WRAPPING UP

Step 1. Why did the father beat the mother?

Step 2. What did the son do when this happened? Notice that he had different responses at different times.

Step 3. What made the mother finally decide to leave home?

Step 4. How did she escape from the car, after the father took off the door knobs?

Step 5. In what ways is violence *learned*?

Step 6. How can a person *unlearn* violence?

Step 7. Have you experienced family violence in your own life or seen it in the life of a close friend or relative? Describe it to someone else if you feel comfortable.

LEARNING STRATEGY

Forming Concepts: Considering new sides to an issue expands your understanding.

Task 4.51 Expanding Your Knowledge

CONSIDERING VARIOUS SIDES OF THE ISSUES

Step 1. In thinking about families, it is important to consider different sides of important issues. It is also important to know your own opinions. After careful consideration, put an "X" below the TRUE column if you believe the statement is true, and put an "X" below the FALSE column if you think the statement is false.

	TRUE	FALSE
1. Arranged marriages are better than marriages that happen through dating.	______	______
2. My family must approve of the person I marry.	______	______
3. I would not marry someone my family did not like.	______	______
4. Financial issues are very important in the choice of a mate.	______	______
5. A formal **dowry** is essential for a marriage.	______	______
6. Divorce is not allowable.	______	______
7. Divorce is okay under certain circumstances, such as **adultery** or physical abuse.	______	______
8. Divorce should be "no fault" and up to the judgment of the partners.	______	______
9. Married women with young children should stay at home.	______	______
10. All married women should stay at home.	______	______
11. Women should go out to work if they want or need to.	______	______
12. Some women are better mothers if they also work outside the home.	______	______
13. Husbands and wives should have equal power.	______	______

Threads

Never go to bed mad.
Stay up and fight.

Comedienne Phyllis Diller

	TRUE	FALSE
14. The husband is the head of the household and should make the key decisions.	______	______
15. Fathers should be stern and have great authority.	______	______
16. The mother makes all the real decisions.	______	______
17. Parents' needs are not as important as children's needs.	______	______
18. Punishment of children should be swift and strong.	______	______
19. Children should be reasoned with, not punished physically.	______	______
20. It is better if the grandparents, aunts, and uncles live together with the rest of the family.	______	______
21. Equality between husband and wife causes divorce.	______	______
22. Rape is merely a sudden sexual act that has little meaning.	______	______
23. Rape is an attempt to dominate another person through sexual force.	______	______
24. Men who rape women deserve to be killed.	______	______
25. Family connections must be very strong if children are to succeed.	______	______
26. People owe their greatest loyalty to their families.	______	______
27. Children should "make it" on their own, so they can show independence.	______	______
28. If children leave home before marriage, this indicates a family problem.	______	______

Step 2. There are no right or wrong answers to many of the statements above, although some are perhaps more clearly correct or incorrect. Your values often dictate whether you believe something is right or wrong, true or false. Keeping that in mind, hold a small group discussion of the answers to the survey above.

Step 3. Now tally the numbers of people that answered TRUE and the number that responded FALSE to each statement. Put the results on the blackboard or on a poster. This is especially interesting if you have people from different cultures participating, but it is eye-opening to discover the **divergence** of opinions even within a single culture.

CULTURAL PATTERN 6: CREATING HAPPIER FAMILIES

Task 4.52 Prelistening

MAKING SUGGESTIONS FOR CHANGE

Write down at least 10 suggestions for change that would create happier families, more balanced gender roles, and less violence.

Task 4.53 Listening

CHECKING OUT THE SUGGESTIONS OF OTHERS

Next you will read two short articles that make concrete suggestions for change. Check your own list to see whether these suggestions are on it. Expand your list.

Your tape has **"Top Seven Problems in Schools"** and **"Three Things Children Need."** From *Familyhood*, pp. 38–39 and 190. Copyright © Lee Salk, 1992. Reprinted by permission of Authors and Artists Group, Inc.

Your tape also has **"Tips for a Happy Marriage."** From *Delicious! Your Magazine of Natural Living*, May/June, 1993, p. 35. Reprinted by permission of New Hope Communications, Inc.

Task 4.54 Postlistening

CONSIDERING CHANGE

Threads

It is dangerous to confuse children with angels.

Sir David Maxwell Fyfe

Step 1. Do you agree or disagree with Dr. Salk's prescriptions for family life and care of children? Why or why not?

Step 2. What are the cultural difficulties in implementing some or all of Dr. Salk's suggestions? How might these difficulties be overcome?

Step 3. Do you agree or disagree with Christopher Aesoph's ideas about improving marriages? Explain.

Step 4. What are the cultural difficulties in implementing some or all of Christopher Aesoph's suggestions? How might these difficulties be overcome?

Step 5. Discuss your responses with people from various cultures. Do they agree or disagree? What are the cultural assumptions that underlie their ideas and yours?

LEARNING STRATEGY

Remembering New Material: Labeling words as culturally "negative" or "positive" concepts might help you remember those words.

Task 4.55 Wordbuilding

ASSESSING THE POSITIVE AND NEGATIVE

The new words in this chapter are charged with many positive and negative values (depending on your culture).

Step 1. To learn the new words, review them several times.
Step 2. Now mark each one according to whether it seems positive or negative, based on your cultural values.

abuse—misuse, harm, injustice
adultery—voluntary sexual intercourse of a married person with a person other than the spouse
agnostic—a person who thinks that nothing can be known about the existence of God
authoritarian—relating to the theory that respect for authority is more important than individual freedom; domineering
awkwardness—clumsiness
bedrock—foundation, basic issue
bistro—the French form of a pub
bribe—a secret gift (usually of money) offered to a person in a position of trust to persuade the person to help the giver
brunette—having dark hair and complexion
confined—limited, kept within limits
cosseting—pampering, overly caring
delegated—having given up (some degree of one's powers) to another
divergence—variation from the norm, difference
dowry—the money, land, or other possessions which a woman brings to her husband under a marriage contract
exaggeration—a step beyond the truth in describing something
exile—banishment or expulsion from one's home or country; or a voluntary living outside one's country
feminology—a made-up word meaning knowledge of women
festering—producing bitter feelings, rankling
festivities—merry-making, gaiety
liturgy—public rites and services of the church
machismo—exaggerated masculinity

mannerisms—affected gestures, habits, manners of speaking, etc.
menial—a domestic servant

NOTE This word has already been used in an earlier chapter as an adjective.

miniature—very small
muddled—confused, unclear
noxious—harmful, corrupting
officialdom—official bureaucracy
oppression—treatment characterized by unjust harshness and tyranny
orthodox—of or conforming to the official, accepted or standard opinions, not heretical or independent
phalanx—a body of people solidly grouped for action
prosecutor—a person who starts legal proceedings against another
psalm—a sacred song
pub—a public house for eating and drinking
sanctified—made holy
serf—a feudal laborer bound to an estate
servitude—slavery, bondage
spindrift—fine spray blown from the surface of water
staggering—shocking, astonishing
superficially—in a manner that does not have any depth
temptress—a woman who tries to persuade someone to do something, especially something that will involve her in a sinful act
tutelage—guardianship, protection, and instruction
VIP—very important person

CHECKING YOUR SUCCESS

Task 4.56 Evaluating

REVIEWING THE OBJECTIVES AND RATING YOURSELF

IT WORKS! Learning Strategy: Assessing Your Ability

Circle YES or NO below.

Can you . . .

- explain at least four key differences in family structures and values around the world? YES NO
- describe how parents and children interact in various cultures? YES NO
- explain how wives and husbands relate to each other in different cultures? YES NO

- tell how women's and men's roles differ culturally? YES NO
- describe how children respond when faced with violence at home? YES NO
- give hints on how to create happier families, more balanced gender roles, and less violence? YES NO
- use many learning strategies to make your studying easier? YES NO

WHERE TO GO FOR MORE INFORMATION

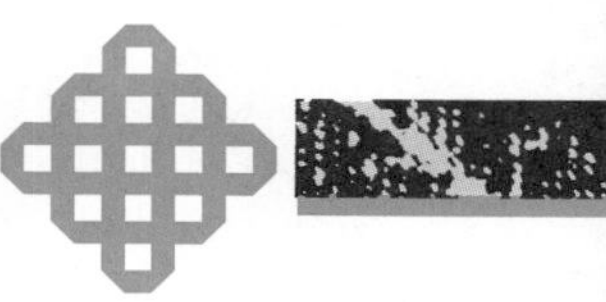

Althen, Gary (1988). *American ways: A guide for foreigners in the United States.* Yarmouth, Me.: Intercultural Press.

Ansley, Leslie (1993, Aug. 13–15). Many teens feel unsafe in school. *USA Today,* p. 1A.

Aries, Philippe (1962). *Centuries of childhood: A social history of family life.* New York: Vintage.

Condon, John C. (1985). *Good neighbors: Communicating with the Mexicans.* Yarmouth, Me.: Intercultural Press.

Courtois, Christine (1988). *Healing the incest wound: Adult survivors in therapy.* New York: W.W. Norton.

Dr. Lee Salk on raising kids in changing times. (1992, Sept. 9) *Family Circle,* pp. 65–66, 70.

Fewer Americans marry (1992, July 29). *News for You,* p. 1.

Gordon, Donna (1993, July/Aug.). What shall we do with our daughters? *The World: The Journal of the Unitarian Universalist Association* 7(4): 26–29.

Herman, Judith Lewis (1981). *Father-daughter incest.* Cambridge: Harvard University Press.

Herman, Judith Lewis (1992). *Trauma and recovery: The aftermath of violence—from domestic abuse to political terror.* New York: Basic Books.

Ingrassia, Michelle (1993, Aug. 30). Endangered family. *Newsweek,* pp. 17–27.

Katchadourian, Herant A. & Lunde, Donald T. (1975). *Fundamentals of human sexuality.* 2nd ed. New York: Holt, Rinehart and Winston.

Kearney, Edward N., Kearney, Mary Ann, & Crandall, JoAnn (1984). *The American way: An introduction to American culture.* Englewood Cliffs, N.J.: Prentice Hall Regents.

Kerber, Linda K. Fighting for a jury of her peers. (1993, Aug. 8) *Miami Herald,* pp. 1C, 5C.

Kornblum, William (1988). *Sociology in a changing world.* New York: Holt, Rinehart and Winston.

Lakoff, George (1987). *Women, fire, and dangerous things: What categories reveal about the mind.* Chicago: University of Chicago Press.

Landsberg, Mitchell (1993, Aug. 29). Battle between the sexes took a sharp turn in Manassas. Associated Press. *Tuscaloosa News,* pp. 2F, 4F.

Le Guin, Ursula K. (1989). *Dancing at the edge of the world: Thoughts on words, women, places.* New York: Harper & Row.

Morganthau, Tom, with Peter Annin, John McCormick, Pat Wingert, Donna Foote, Howard Manly, & Patricia King (1992, Mar. 9). It's not just New York . . . Big cities, small towns: More and more guns in younger and younger hands. *Newsweek,* pp. 25–29.

New findings on vicious wife beaters (1993, Aug. 27). *USA Today,* p. 4D.

Nordland, Ron. Deadly lessons (1992, Mar. 9). *Newsweek,* pp. 22–24.

Salk, Lee (1992). *Familyhood.* New York: Simon & Schuster.

Scanzoni, J. (1978). *Sex roles, women's work, and marital conflict.* Lexington, Mass.: Lexington Books.

Scarcella, Robin (1990). *Teaching language minority students in the multicultural classroom.* Englewood Cliffs, N.J.: Prentice Hall.

Skolnik, Arlene, & Jerome Skolnik (eds.) (1980). *Families in transition.* Boston: Little, Brown.

Spack, Ruth (1994). *The international story: An anthology with guidelines for reading and writing about fiction.* New York: St. Martin's.

Stone, Elizabeth (1988). *Black sheep and kissing cousins: How our family stories shape us.* New York: Penguin.

Tan, Amy (1989). *The Joy Luck Club.* New York: Ivy Books.

Afterword

NEW PATTERNS EMERGE

In this book you have seen many patterns of culture. In Chapter 1 you explored everyday culture and sophisticated culture, the cultural iceberg, steps in cultural understanding, culture shock, and people's experiences in a new culture. Chapter 2 was a sometimes serious, sometimes fanciful flight into time and space, key patterns in any culture. In Chapter 3 you delved into touch, gesture, posture, and gaze and discovered many customs related to these physical aspects of culture. Chapter 4 brought you home to the foundation of culture: the modern family, with its pleasures, pains, and ever-evolving patterns.

With this book you have learned a great deal about your own cultural identity. Your sense of yourself as a human being is grounded in your home culture. No matter how much you travel, you see yourself primarily through the lens of your culture.

New patterns—broad-scale compassion, mercy, justice, and concern—can emerge for you as an individual, for your culture, and for all cultures. These new patterns can evolve through through cross-cultural experiences, through learning to communicate in a language that is not the mother tongue, and through working internationally to solve human problems.

The Soros Foundation, the Peace Corps, the American Friends Service Committee, and various cultural and educational branches of many governments are working to create new, positive patterns of cultural understanding. Yet perhaps individuals, not agencies, have the most important role in contributing to greater cross-cultural harmony. You have taken your first step by reading this book. The world awaits you. Look for cultural patterns wherever you go.